Caleb S. Weeks

Songs of the Morning

original and selected

Caleb S. Weeks

Songs of the Morning
original and selected

ISBN/EAN: 9783337265762

Printed in Europe, USA, Canada, Australia, Japan

Cover: Foto ©Thomas Meinert / pixelio.de

More available books at **www.hansebooks.com**

SONGS OF THE MORNING.

ORIGINAL AND SELECTED.

By CALEB S. WEEKS.

IN TWO VOLUMES.

VOL. I. ORIGINAL—INCLUDING RESPONSES TO OLD HYMNS, AND OLD HYMNS IN RESPONDING VERSIONS.

VOL. II. SELECTIONS.

Vol. I.

NEW YORK:
THE TRUTH SEEKER OFFICE,
21 CLINTON PLACE.
1883.

TO ALL WHO,
SOUL-INSPIRED BY THE LIGHT OF
OUR MANHOOD'S DAWNING MORNING,
WOULD IN SONG GIVE VENT
TO THEIR NEWLY-AWAKENING LIFE,
BUT ARE NOT YET ABLE TO GIVE IT
BETTER EXPRESSION.

INTRODUCTORY REMARKS.

There is, I believe, no more urgent need among those who are awaking from the night of superstition than that the newly-toned melody of their souls should find free expression in songs which honor and aid, rather than abase and check the rational faculties, thus inspiring the emotions while freeing, enlightening, and exalting them. This need is greatest where consciousness of it is least. Songs are wanted which shall help intellect and intuition in their efforts to unite their counterpart elements so as to form completed manly reason—reason which need not war upon the soul's emotions in order to defend its own existence, but which, clear-sighted, can see through all mythologic mists, and readily separate living truths from the dead, decaying dogmas which ecclesiasticisms would retain with them. Then it will not only clear and enlarge its own field, but also expand and intensify all the spiritual sensibilities and powers, making all the human faculties co-workers for truth and human happiness.

Many of those who have consciously rejected the dogmas of old superstition are yet in the acute stage of the outer intellect's strife for liberty to unfold reason's commencing life. Perceiving how effective a use ecclesiastical institutions and powers make of singing to enslave the emotions to superstition, they half-suppose that music and emotion united must be a foe to intellectual freedom, and thus they leave this powerful means of Nature's grace to work against them, while they are chilled and benumbed for want of it.

Tho' some have logically perceived, and some, not so seeing, have, in moments of inspiration, intuitively discerned the relation of such music to their needs, and poured forth their souls in song, yet most of the religiously freed are still shivering amid the fetid emanations of decomposing dogmas, which they linger to fight, as if they were living foes, instead of burrying dogmatic authority and the dead moralisms, its fortifications, and coming where the Morning rays may clear the senses and enliven the emotions, thus aiding the growth of the living religion and real moral philosophy.

Believing that more of these would see the true character of song, and use this powerful soul-vivifier as their own, if melody, harmony and emotion were united with truthful, elevating thought, I have here put forth some of my own chirpings, hoping they may somewhat help to serve this purpose, and have made a selection from our Morning Songsters' warblings for the second volume of this work.

Among my own, many are responses to old hymns, and some are responding versions. Some of the old hymns slightly changed in words, again become live spiritual truths, as they were in their original form to the age that thus embodied them in germs of thought. I have retained for the new songs, selections, and the old as resurrected and *re*-newed in responses, the soul-stirring tunes which the waking spiritual emotions set to the crude, half-awakened thought of the old hymns. Melody is immortal, and should have a body of living thought. It needs well-formed thought, but can work with the defective if it is vital enough to serve the ever-living emotions. It will be true to itself, and to life.

It ever makes the incongruous, dead and disorganizing conditions more apparent. The old sectaries are partially feeling this, and, as they lose the spiritual vitality, they yield up the thought-life of their earlier songs; but as, for church-consistency's sake, they cannot disown the words, they drop the spiritual tunes, in which their life chiefly consisted, inventing such new ones as, by their inappropriateness of emotion, make spiritless the words which have become thoughtless. Thus they are resigning to the spiritually revivified the tunes which they delighted in when the words expressed living ideals and served living faith's cravings. It is appropriate that we accept the surrender.

Let us ALL sing! "Sing in the spirit and with the understanding!" When we have songs which well express the soul's highest conceptions of living truth, instead of dead or dying forms of infantile faith, we shall rapidly learn to do so.

If my own and *some* of the selections are not a high order of poetry, they express in some degree the sentiments of the live, evolving, natural faith. They may have remains of old befogged thought tinging them, for the Morning Dawn, in awakening souls to song, inspires with truths before it can make them perfectly clear to the eye; and, moreover, where they are clearly seen, the feebleness of spoken language, even tho' we press larger meaning into words, must give written thought some of its old shading as well as its vagueness. This may be distasteful to those who see surface-distortions but not the glory of truth under such partial vailings. Who can avoid this difficulty?

SONGS OF THE MORNING.

VOL. I.

ORIGINAL, INCLUDING RESPONSES

TO

OLD HYMNS,

AND

RESPONDING VERSIONS.

INDEX OF SUBJECTS.

FIRST LINES OF SONGS.

INDEX OF TUNES.

These, and other tunes suitable for these songs, may be found in the old tune books used in congregational singing, most of them in the "Psalms of Life," "The Spiritual Harp," "The Revivalist," or the "Methodist Hymnal," published in 1878 as a new revision. The latter, perhaps, has more of them than any other book in popular use, for Methodism still considerably serves religious emotion, where fuller Morning gospel is unknown.

SONGS OF THE MORNING.

VOL I.—PART I.

ORIGINAL AND NEW.

1 FAITH DISCERNS THE MORNING.

C. M. *Tune—Coronation.*

There comes on every passing breeze
  New sounds of joyous cheer:
The waking warblers in the trees
  Proclaim the dawn is here.

The flowers, responding, fill the air
  With melody-perfume—
With welcomes open everywhere
  As morning rays illume.

Faith's vital germ within the rose,
  In birds with instinct-power,
As day-beams feeblest rays disclose,
  Discerns the morning hour:

Tho' fogs may thickly gather round,
  And seem to vail the day,
Exulting, confidence profound
  Maintains its perfect sway.

Through all the gloom which thus assails
  It sees the dawning gleams,
And triumphs over all that vails
  Its view of morning beams.

And shall our faith, in drowsy plight,
  By vapors blinded be?
No; let us rouse, and morning light
  Through all the mists we'll see!

2 'TIS MORNING: WE AWAKE.

C. M. *Tune—Antioch.*

'Tis morning! and our nature, now,
  Awakes from dogma-dreams;
And, tho' the vapors vail the brow,
  Begins to catch the gleams.

'Tis morning! all despairing creeds
  Of superstition-fright
Are fading, and our human needs
  Begin to claim their right.

'Tis morning! see! man's waking sense
  Now half disowns his fears,
While misty thought would drive from hence
  The light which dawns and cheers.

'Tis morning! e'en the darkest mind
  Some lighting rays has found;
And intuition strives to find
  His nature's higher ground.

'Tis morning! shout the word around!
  The mists now break and clear;
Man soon shall see, with joy profound,
  His God is with him here.

---

3 NATURE SHAPES ANEW. C. M.

How beautifully in our sight
  All nature shapes anew,
When mists no more distort the light
  Of morning's opening view.

The "evils," which have vexed us long,
  Before us now appear
As blessings to inspire our song
  Of lively morning cheer.

We see that every seeming ill
Is goodness misapplied—
That pains are teachers to reveal
The laws which joys provide.

That all of life in earth and skies
The laws divine express,
As ripening fruits before our eyes
Transform their bitterness.

O joy! we see in open light
All nature shape anew—
See heaven unfolding in our sight
Through nature's laws so true!

We gladly would the sight display
To every human eye:
We cry to all: "Awake! 'Tis day!
The mists and darkness fly!"

---

4 HEAVEN UNFOLDING HERE. C. M.

Lo, what a glorious sight appears
As misty darkness flies—
The new evolving earth and heavens
Take form before our eyes!

The judgment-fire, now spreading round,
Old error's world consumes—
Its states and churches melt away
As morning light illumes.

Old despots, trembling, seek to hide
Beneath their mountain-wrongs;
Their rocks and mountains flee away
At manhood's waking songs.

We see that here our God resides,
And on our lowly race,

As through the highest heavens above,
Sheds his abounding grace

And those whose *outer* senses fail
The work to clearly see
Find *inner* wake; and angels aid
Their nature's life to free.

The breaking mists will soon disperse,
And all, with vision clear,
Behold, 'mid "hells" consuming round,
Our heaven unfolding here.

---

5 THE TRUE MESSIAH NOW APPEARS

C. M. *Tune—Coronation.*

The true Messiah now appears
In manhood's morning dawn;
Ideals childish faith reveres
Are from our view withdrawn:

The fancied bleeding sacrifice
No longer justice seems;
The real justice greets our eyes
While waking from our dreams:

The opening senses catch the view
Through all the mists around,
Of Love and Wisdom—God (the true)—
Who in our life is found.

Incarnated in man we see
The all-perfecting love,
With saving grace, his spirit free
For higher heavens above.

Distorting vapors roll away,
And. to our joyous eyes,

Truth straightens all the warped display
  Which seemed destructive lies.

We joy in manhood's-morning beams,
  And our Messiah here;
Exult! the faith-distorting dreams
  Give place to vision clear.

ADORATION AND TRUST OF NATURE.

C. M.

O Nature, we adore thy name,
  In joy we dimly see
Thy laws that built our wondrous frame
  Of living energy.

The partial-outline view reveals
  Thy loving wisdom's sway,
While yet the lingering mist conceals
  The full and clear display.

We cast our opening eyes around,
  And beauties on us beam;
We look within—a vast profound
  Of mental forces gleam.

In wonder lost, we faintly scan
  Thy active building power,
Which from the clod constructs the man,
  Whose thoughts to heaven can tower.

He grasps the mighty forces round,
  And turns them to his use;
Gains wisdom's light and freedom's ground
  From blunders and abuse.

The love and wisdom infinite
  In Nature's laws we see;
And rest securely in the might
  That serves so perfectly.

7 FAITH'S FOUNDATION AND GRASP.

C. M.

As dawning light increases round,
And darkening mists grow thin,
We wake from superstition-woes—
The terror-dream of sin.

We see eternal wisdom blends,
In counterparting flow,
With mother-love—a perfect God—
And rules above, below.

We see our God on every soul
Bestow pefecting grace,
Revealing to each opened eye
His ever-smiling face.

The conscience, wounded by the sting
Which false ideals give,
Within the light finds healing balm
To make the dying live.

The loves here know their union true
With the Divinity,
And find the free inflowing life
From morbid passions free.

Faith now, exulting, firmly stands
On knowledge as its base,
And reaches forth untrammeled hands,
Which grasp the boundless space.

---

8 THE SOUL'S FREEDOM. C.M.

Now, in the opening morning rays,
We wake to nature's prayer,
And join the joyous songs of praise
Which greet us everywhere.

The warming glow new vigor brings,
  The scales fall from our eyes,
Faith shakes the mildew from her wings,
  And, soaring, mounts the skies.

The intuitions learn to trust
  Their soul-activities,
And reason, rising from the dust,
  The laws-eternal sees.

They join their powers, and thus explore
  The hights till now untrod,
While leading onward, just before,
  We see our nature's God.

Old superstition now in vain
  Declares its haughty claims
To dictate to our life, again,
  Its duties and its aims.

Since in the light, with nature's God,
  Our powers could freedom know
E'en when in discord's hells we've trod
  To soothe our fellows' woe.

---

9 THE FREE SOUL'S NEW DELIGHTS.

C. M.

Our souls awake to new delights
  In reason's morning rays;
The ills which once produced affright
  We find inciting praise.

In nature's God a friend we see,
  Whose wisdom never fails;
Whose love for all is working free,
  And evermore prevails.

We see that all in earth and heaven
  But serve for human weal;

That pains, to follies kindly given,
  The laws of joy reveal.

Faith's eyes, now opened, well can see,
  As storms the heavens clear,
That sorrow-tempests serve to free
  The spirits atmosphere:

That racking-blasts the vigor nerve
  Of roots and branches, all
To broaden out and better serve
  Enlarging being's call.

Thus, free from all desponding fear,
  To "hells" our work is given;
And faith beholds, with lively cheer,
  Each changing to a heaven.

---

10 TENDERNESS TOWARD OLD ERRORS.

C. M.

My waking powers, why linger ye
  To fondle childish creeds?
The light has come to set you free;
  It calls for manly deeds.

Why when the truth, inspiring, brings
  Its energizing power,
Should aspiration clog her wings
  With toys of childhood's hour?

Why, love fraternal, in thy flow
  To friends, in tender play,
Preserve the darkening mists which so
  Obscure their nature's day?

The morning light, when deepening round,
  Calls forth from every rill
The vailing mists to save the ground
  From frost's benumbing chill;

Then lifts them, and o'er hill and plain
  Their golden linings throw
New light and warmth, to serve the grain,
  And gladden all below.

Thus doth the sunlight of the mind
  Old error-mists control,
And with its breaking vapors find
  How to illume the soul.

---

11 HERE FIND THY GOD. C. M.

Creed-darkened soul, this is the place
  Where thou thy God mayest find!
All nature shows his loving face
  To the enlightened mind.

His smiling features on us beam
  From earth and sea and skies;
The grossest clod reflects the gleam;
  The founts are love-lit eyes.

When in the deepest soul-distress
  Of superstition-fear,
Unrecognized, his kindly grace
  Still serves thy life to cheer.

While ancient dogmas, deemed divine,
  Are fading from thy view,
Love's life thy nature doth refine,
  And gives a faith more true.

Trust inner light while outer sense
  With doubt and sadness strives!
The darkening mists will pass from hence,
  Illumined faith survives.

12 DEATH IS RESURRECTION. C. M.

Why should we drop a sorrow-tear
  When life's evolving flow
The vestments sheds which served it here
  Awhile in scenes below?

Are not all forms of life we see
  Ascending thus, to gain,
In larger measure and degree,
  What serves their higher plane?

When nature's God with beckoning calls,
  Life rises him to greet;
And while the husk, now useless, falls,
  New circles there complete:

The solid rocks dissolve to free
  The soul of motion there;
And vegetation yields, we see,
  Sensation-germs they bear.

Perfected, then, through long careers
  Of sensuous nature's flow,
They ever rise, until appears
  The child of God below.

Thus man—the spirit—ever true
  To life-perfecting laws,
Ascends, and, in relations new,
  Outworks the perfect cause.

---

13 DUST TO DUST. C. M.

Now, Mother Earth, receive again
  The dust thy love hath lent;
It wrought full well, e'en when in pain,
  To aid the soul's ascent.

'Twas Nature's loving life in thee
That built the wondrous form,
And filled with vital energy
Which served through every storm.

When feeble outer senses failed
To see their nature's need,
The inner vigor's work prevailed,
And from obstructions freed.

And pain but nerved its efforts more
To thoroughly subdue
Whatever placed itself before
The powers of life so true.

And, tho' the senses' struggle seemed
To dim the spirit's eyes,
From inmost fountains ever streamed
Its real life-supplies.

Outworn, it frees, through transient pain,
The soul for new ascent;
So, Mother Earth, receive again
The dust thy love hath lent.

---

14 DEATH, LIFE'S CONDUCTOR. C. M.

In morning light, now spreading wide,
From dark distortions free,
No more the life-conductor guide
A "demon foe" we see.

The "monster" of our nature's night
Our greatest friend appears;
We wake from superstition fright—
From all benumbing fears.

We see the all-conducting hand,
In universal lead,
Assisting life where fields more grand
May serve its higher need.

What tho' awhile, in misty view,
 We stumble, causing pain,
And, unripe vestments breaking through,
 Life's freedom thus must gain?

Our race's slight and transient woes
 Reveal the laws of joy;
Death aids our triumph o'er the foes
 That would our bliss alloy.

---

15 HAIL, MANHOOD'S MORNING STAR!

L. M.

Hail, morning star of manhood's day,
 Who, beckoning, leads the dawning rays!
Thy light on our long-darkened way,
 Our nature's path of life displays.

Our race long struggled on in pain
 Through superstion's starless night;
Now morning-beams flow o'er the plain,
 And quicken the enfeebled sight.

The flashes of our nature's life,
 As through the night and mists they shone,
Distorted, seemed a "horid strife"
 Of passions fired by "ill" alone.

For help divine we loudly prayed,
 Yet struggled 'gainst the answering power;
Deemed it a dreadful "demon" raid,
 Which joy and hope would soon devour.

But now thy glorious morning-gleams
 Dispel forebodings and affright,
And herald the approaching beams
 Which all our race shall fully light.

Our waking souls, exulting, sing
  The glories which thy beams display;
And to all peoples' view would bring
  The morning star of manhood's day.

---

16 THE DAWNING DEEPENS. L. M.

The dawning deepens all around,
Dispersing all the gloom profound,
And all the phantoms of the night
Transform within the morning light.

Before our opening, wondering eyes
We see abounding life-supplies;
And all the dreaded "evils" prove
The angels of all-conquering love.

The seeming pitfalls in our path,
And "goblin forms," and " flashing wrath,"
We see were but the misty-view
Distortions of the good and true.

We shrink no more in trembling fear
When transient sorrow-clouds appear;
Hope, standing on foundations sure,
Towers where the light is cloudless, pure.

And faith, well based on law divine,
Sees God and Nature's powers combine
To aid our life's evolving flow
Completed harmony to know.

Well may we, then, with joy profound,
Exult as light thus spreads around
And "demons" of the gloomy night
Transform to angels in our sight.

17 OPEN DAY WILL GIVE SMILING SKIES. L. M.

As dawning beams of coming day
The gloom and darkness drive away,
The frosty chains of error bend,
Then melt to vapors and ascend.

As gathering clouds, they now reveal
The light they once did so conceal—
With golden linings, see, they glow.
And coming sunshine on us throw.

And tho' at times they close again,
And shadows dark cast o'er the plain,
We know that soon their darkening power
Will yield to morning's lighting hour.

We learn that tho' they sometimes pour
Their drenching floods the landscape o'er,
New energy from this will spring
To aid the flowers in blossoming:

That tho' the winds, untamed, may rage,
And war destructive seem to wage,
The morning shoots will still prevail,
And strengthen in the surging gale.

The tempests of our nature's night
Grow feebler in our morning light;
We fear no more; we know that day
With smiling skies will cheer our way.

---

18 JOY IN MORNING TRANSFORMATIONS. L. M.

In morning light we joy to-day,
  Tho' long, in superstition-fright,
We strove against each dawning ray,
  And cherished human nature's night.

The fogs disperse which long have been
  Distorting all our eyes perceived;
And fancied "evils" now are seen
  The friends which human ills relieved.

Each "pit of woe" we quaked to view,
  We find is but a misty vale;
We wake in light to life anew,
  Assured that life and love prevail.

Our God, we see, abides with man,
  And loving smiles illume his face;
While pain but works his kindly plan,
  And shows the law and means of grace.

We see our blunders—"sins"—are calls
  Which bring these monitors to teach,
That by their aid through childhood-falls
  True manhood-balance we may reach.

The "demons" of our frightful dreams
  Are seen to be our nature's friends;
The hells transform with heavenly gleams;
  The morning comes! the darkness ends!

---

19 THE LAW OF DIVINE GRACE. L. M.

In solemn joy our spirits see
  The natures which in darkness cower
Explode in passions wild, which free
  From superstion's dwarfing power.

The vital vices break the sway
  Of "moral" fancies that enslave;
With seeming wrecks they strew our way,
  But wield the vigor which will save.

While outer sense in sadness strives
  To check their work of "woe" and "waste,"

While they embitter much our lives,
  Faith sweetens well the cup we taste.

Our opening eyes in morning light,
  As scattering dogma-mists grow thin,
Awake from morbid-dream affright
  Of hopeless "evil"—fancied "sin."

We see the "monster" of our fear
  Is Nature's life, which wounds to heal;
Who calls and monitors appear—
  The pains—which nature's laws reveal.

Faith in the light accepts with joy
  The law of God and Nature's grace;
And would our growing powers employ
  To aid its growth within our race.

---

20 DIVINE GRACE WORKS IN US. L. M.

As day-beams, deepening round our heads,
  In ever-brightening glory shine,
We see that God and Nature spreads
  O'er all the earth the grace divine:

That streams of loving life-supply
  The universe of worlds embrace;
While the great fountain, never dry,
  Is boundless as the realms of space.

That the immortal energy
  And laws and powers of its control
Are working ever mightily
  In each unfolding human soul.

That all the pains and sorrows known
  Are merely ripples of the tide;
While Nature in our hands hath thrown
  The power upon its crests to ride.

What fuller gospel could be given
  Than that we here, on earth, may know
A real soul-supplying heaven
  Evolving in our nature's flow?

Ho, all ye trembling sons of fear,
  From dreamy-terror now arise!
Your heaven is building, God is here,
  Awake, and open wide your eyes!

---

21 THE ALL-PERFECTING PROVIDENCE. L.M.

O life-inspiring Love Divine,
The life of Nature all is thine!
How strange to our half-waking sense
Thy wondrous ways of providence!

Our spirit-senses first in play
From fleshly trammels break away,
And lift our aspiration-eyes
In dauntless strife to scale the skies.

Then when our soaring energy,
In sense of spirit-mastery,
Inflates to pharisaic pride,
The p..ssion-powers its checks provide:

In vice-explosions thus the soul
Breaks loose again from false control,
Until the physical regains
A power which blinded flight restrains.

In vain crude aspiration chides;
In vain the sense its voice derides;
Each nobly serves till, ripe and free,
Our powers can work in harmony.

O life-inspiring Love Divine,
How doth thy perfect wisdom shine
In thus subjecting soul and sense
To thy perfecting providence!

---

22 MORNING GOSPEL'S HARSHER TONES. L.M.

New gospel tones of heavenly cheer,
As morning dawns, salute the ear—
Old "demon" voices "threatening woe,"
In loving accents on us flow.

The harshest which our ears have heard,
And those which most our fears have stirred,
Tell us, in most heroic strain,
Their work is love, and not in vain:

The tempest raging round our door,
Through all its seeming "threatening" roar
Says, "See! my mission is not death—
I purify your vital breath!"

The ocean's billows, when they rise,
And seem to madly war with skies,
Say, "Thus the waters and the air
For life-support we well prepare."

The earthquake, seeming to devour,
But speaks of life's resistless power
O'er what at times would interfere
'Twixt breathing earth and atmosphere.

The thunder, rolling in the sky,
Proclaims that Nature's life-supply,
While in its universal play
Will all obstructions sweep away.

23 AMEN TO "DISCORD" TONES. L. M.

"Amen!" we say—no more we fear
The morning's harshest tones to hear;
Tho' some discordant seem to be,
We know they tune to harmony.

The earth will soon, in open light,
Behold her skies serene and bright;
Her vital powers in perfect play,
And no obstructions in the way.

Then elements shall war no more
In earthquake-shocks and thunder's roar;
Nor racking passions madly roll
Across the ripened human soul.

We joy in all the conquering power
Of manhood's clearing morning hour;
Let equilibrium-strifes appear
We say, "Amen!" we never fear!

The vapors floating o'er the plains,
The gathering clouds and falling rains,
The bubbling springs and streamlets' flow
Respond, "Amen! its love we know!"

The skies with brighter smiles inspire
Each thing of life with vital fire;
Awake, O sleepers! you will then
The chorus join and shout "Amen!"

---

24 NATURE REVEALS HER LORD.
L. M.

All nature's life reveals her Lord;
His love and wisdom's perfect word:
Where'er we look, where'er we turn,
His power and glory we discern:

The surging storms, the smiling skies,
The earth with blooming life-supplies,
The solid ground and viewless air
His active presence well declare.

Old ocean ever makes it plain;
Its rising vapor, falling rain,
Refining wrestlings with the skies,
And mountain-springs its fount supplies.

All vital are with life divine;
Their great constructive works combine,
And reproduce on higher plan
All forms and forces joined in man.

Then tho' young forming-power may find
Its labors checked while sense is blind,
'Twill light and equilibrium gain,
Altho' it strives awhile in pain.

Then let us work and never cower
Before the troubles of the hour;
In nature's faith sublimely rise,
And taste her proffered life-supplies.

---

25 GOSPEL REVEALED IN NATURE.

L. M.

Our God his gospel-truth makes known
In every star, in every stone;
His love and wisdom well displays
In worms, that glow, and suns, that blaze.

Throughout our wondrous earth we see
It well unfold in lessons free;
In ocean's depths, and earth, and air,
Through law unfolding everywhere.

And clearest in the vital flow
Through living forms, his law we know;
Here law and gospel, one, divine,
In golden letters ever shine.

In man the brightest page we find—
His wondrous body, heart, and mind,
Express the all-perfecting laws,
And life's relation to its cause.

Its perfect language all may hear:
It flows in accents ever clear
From loves in unobstructed play;
While *blunders* this in part display.

Well understood, it tunes the soul
To harmony's divine control—
From woes and discords fully saves,
And from the fear which man enslaves.

---

26 THE MOUNTAINS' LESSON OF FAITH.

L. M.

When I behold the mountains rise
And boldly kiss the glowing skies,
My soul the lesson thence derives
That earth and heaven unite their lives.

I see they gain the freest play
Of heavenly breathings day by day;
And learn that fullest blessings greet
The faith that *rises* these to meet.

I learn he best his God reveres
Who spurns all self-abasing fears—
Whose filial love exalts his head
To catch the blessings on it shed.

That we should rise in manly might
Where no dark mists of error's night
Contract the soul to grace divine,
Which would exalt, enlarge, refine:

That faith in our own nature's dower,
From God and Nature, is the power
Whose mighty inspirations move
Confiding arms to grasp their love.

Avaunt! then, all ye faithless fears
Of superstition's darkened years!
The life of God is serving mine!
I rise to meet the grace divine!

---

27 THE ENLIGHTENED SOUL NEVER FEARS. L. M.

When o'er our nature's vision lower
  The darkening clouds, with seeming frown,
We know 'tis but the coming shower
  Which God and Nature's grace pours down.

Who once has pierced the vailing mists,
  And God and Nature's features seen,
Finds that their light doth still assist,
  Tho' raging tempests intervene.

Faith sees the law, and rests secure
  On nature's equilibrium-flow—
He knows the providence is sure;
  That joyous ripeness 'twill bestow.

He braves the blasts which broaden out
  His being's roots in Nature's ground,
And spreads confiding arms about
  The wrestling tempest struggling round.

He rises up in peril's hour,
  And danger grapples, thus to mend;
And finds his nature wields the power
  To make each "threatening" foe a friend.

A "saviour," an incarnate God,
  He finds at work within his frame;
And knows that manhood's path well trod,
  Secures salvation in his name.

THE AWAKENING BEGINS.

L. M. *Tune—Old Hundred.*

Tho' darkness long has vailed the earth,
  And despots ruled through many years,
Fair liberty shall soon have birth;
  The dawn of day at length appears.

The eastern sky begins to glow;
  See, brighter grows the silvery gleams!
The heavens above and earth below
  Now feel the sunlight's coming beams.

Birds chirp around, o'er hills and dales
  Life-movement sounds salute the ear;
Man feels the light, nor longer quails
  With dreamy soul-benumbing fear.

The frightened hords of tyrants quake
  While now, before their wondering eyes,
The working masses start, and wake,
  And in the strength of manhood rise.

Monopoly shall soon give way,
  And hide its horrid demon-face,
No more on earth to hold the sway;
  And justice then shall take its place.

Then lift your joyous banners high!
  Exalt your standard everywhere!

The day of triumph draweth nigh,
  Equality to all declare!

---

29 THE MORNING VIEW AND LESSONS.

C. P.M

O morning light, what lessons grand
Thy beams reveal on every hand,
  Instructive, bright and clear!
They spread the hills and valleys o'er;
They strew each road-side; crowd each door,
  With real gospel-cheer.

Unfolding revelations flow,
And on each open soul bestow
  The power to truly see
Great Nature's all-unfolding laws,
And that the all-unfolding cause
  Works ever perfectly.

We see one principle of life
Outworks through all the seeming strife
  Till harmony prevails—
That the divine formation-plan
Works, from the clod, till it in man
  The spirit life unvails;

That all the "hells" earth's children know
Are from the ever-conquering flow
  Of Nature's laws of joy;
That with obstructions cast aside
They will a heaven for all provide
  Of perfect life-employ.

O joyous view in morning beams!
O that we could from morbid dreams
  Wake all the light to know!

Then should we find, through every land,
All sorrow cease, all joys expand—
A heaven begun below.

---

30 A LESSON FROM THE DEW-DROP.

C. P. M.

Tho' morning light shone round my way
And warmed my life to freer play,
I felt a strange distress—
Beloved fellows failed to see;
We could not interchange the free
Fraternal soul-caress.

In yearnings, seeming unsupplied,
I prayed: O Morning Light, provide
The needed love-supplies;
Or if, with interchanging flow,
True life-support we each bestow,
Reveal it to my eyes.

Then, to my yearning nature's prayer,
An answering voice upon the air
In incense-music came—
It said: "The interchange-supply"
Works, tho' unseen by outer eye;
Withhold your childish blame."

I looked, and on a blooming rose,
In joyous, satisfied repose,
A sparkling dew-drop shone,
And, to my spirit's inner ear,
Spake on the words of morning cheer
In clear exulting tone:

It said: "Behold! in morning hour
I seem unnoticed by the flower—
It cannot with me blend;

And I, to those who dimly see,
Seem rounding up myself to be
A self-supplying friend.

"To our own life each being true,
The more the others' help renew,
E'en tho' unconsciously:
I moisture give, and light supply,
And gain perfume, with which I fly,
And fragrance bear to thee."

---

31 NOW WE KNOW THE ANGELS.

C. P. M.

Hail, angel friends! our opening eyes
Your presence now can recognize;
For, in the dawning beams,
You've banished all the blighting fears
Of superstition's night of years—
You've roused us from our dreams.

Tho' long appeared our gloomy night,
And soul-benumbing was the fright
Its morbid dreamings gave,
The glowing, warming light-supply
On bounding veins and open eye,
From its effects can save.

As opening light more fully flows,
And free illumination throws
Upon our yearning souls,
The mighty realms of boundless space
We see are realms of loving grace,
Which evermore controls.

We see that law-divine endears,
And kindred souls, in all the spheres,
Unites in genial love;

That fellowship's outreaching need,
Whate'er obstructions may impede,
  Will ever master prove.

Oh, angel friends! our darkened eyes
Saw you as "demon" enemies,
  Who sought our bliss to blight;
We thought true angels only sent
When special grace Almighty meant
  Some favorite to light.

But you have striven unceasingly,
Since feeblest dawn, to make us see,
  And now have gained success;
Your fellowship at last we know,
And would that its unhindered flow
  Should all our fellows bless.

---

32 OUR SOULS AWAKE. S. M.

Oh, joy! our souls awake
  As morning light appears;
In morbid dreams no more we quake
  With blood-stagnating fears.

The blinding mists, behold!
  Grow thinner day by day;
And nature's fields to us unfold,
  Which long in darkness lay.

The breaking mists oft show
  From all distortions free,
The life of love at work below
  In true divinity.

And then our God is seen
  To look with smiling face
On all of life, no thing too mean
  To share his loving grace.

Altho' an angry frown
  Once seemed to shade his brow,
The beaming love—his perfect crown,
  Is undistorted now.

We joy in morning beams!
  Our nature's night is o'er!
Our souls awake! the morbid dreams
  Our life-streams chill no more!

---

33 WELCOME MORNING LIGHT. S. M.

Oh, welcome, Morning Light!
  We joy to see thee here—
To see the gloomy shades of night
  Disperse and disappear.

Our waking spirits' life,
  In densest darkness, long
Has groped in earnest stumbling-strife
  With superstition's throng.

We yearned with strong desire
  For light to cheer our way,
Yet deemed a "foul, infernal fire,"
  The first-seen rays of day.

When intuition caught
  A reason-lighting gleam,
The soul's aspiring impulse fought
  The soul-illuming beam.

But light increased apace,
  And opened wide our eyes;
And now we call on all our race
  To share the heavenly prize.

34 THE FREE SOUL'S GLORIOUS VIEW.

S. M.

How glorious appears
The smiling earth and skies
When, free from superstition-fear,
We look with open eyes.

The zephyrs, breathing low,
The tempests, raging 'round,
Proclaim the equilibrium-flow
Of Nature's love profound.

In perfect law expressed,
We see its power employ
A wisdom which its fruits has blessed
With powers of ripening-joy.

---

35 OUR GOD'S CENTRAL WORK. S.M.

Our nature's God proclaims
His life is love alone;
His wisdom claims no pompous names,
His power, no monarch's throne.

Our human nature's life
His centering powers combine;
And, through its seeming blunder-strife,
Evolves the life divine.

Ye timid, trembling souls,
His all-perfecting grace
Through all his works to all outrolls,
Through all the realms of space.

Then cast aside your fears,
And open wide your eyes;
See! morning's dawning light appears;
It spreads o'er all the skies.

36 THE MORNING CONCERT. S. M.

A morning concert, grand,
Outrolls from earth and skies;
It says: "O man! within your hand
Are all your life-supplies."

This is the gospel true,
For which our souls have yearned;
We hail it now, tho' long, in view
Distorted, this we spurned.

Now joyously our souls
Incline the willing ear;
And from the tropics to the poles
We fain would spread its cheer.

---

37 THE ANGELS JOIN OUR SONG. S. M.

The angels join our song,
And, with exulting breath,
The joyous morning notes prolong
Of "victory in death!"

We give the welcome hand;—
Our morbid fears are o'er;—
The fancied "demons" 'round us stand—
The loved ones gone before.

We hail the grand surprise
Which crowns the light-display;
Ye sleeping friends, awake! arise!
Behold, 'tis dawning day!

---

38 JOYS NEVER PERISH. S. M.

No real, vital joy
Can ever fade away;

Tho' clouds may vail and grief alloy,
  At last it gains the day:

It wakes to new career,
  And on the memory
Paints glowing hues of blooming cheer,
  Which from all sadness free.

Ye trembling souls who shrink,
  O'erwhelmed by sorrow-waves,
Your life prevails; you cannot sink;
  The God within you saves.

---

39 RELIGION'S REVIVAL. S. M.

We see thy work revive,
  O Nature! in this hour—
The powers of soul, long torpid, strive
  'Gainst superstition's power.

The dawning light, so true,
  Which reaches everywhere,
Wakes human souls to life anew,
  And nature's labor-prayer.

The germs of spirit power
  Are warmed through dogma's clod,
By morning beams, and, every hour,
  Rise to the light of God.

Man's sense of human worth
  Breaks through the servile fear;
No more his goodness and his earth
  As "filthy rags" appear.

The priestly despots cower;
  Old persecution quails;
And 'neath hypocrisy their power
  But partially prevails.

Soon, in the open light,
All, well revived, shall know
Salvation from the shriveling blight
Which superstitions throw.

---

40 A LESSON FROM THE ROSE. S.M.

I asked the fragrant rose:
What lesson dost thou bring—
What morning truth dost thou disclose
In thy bright blossoming?

Its voice, in sweet perfume,
Responding, then replied:
"My fragrant cheer and lighting bloom
To all are now supplied:

"My healing balm I shed
On those who trample me,
E'en while I trip the heedless tread,
My threatened life to free.

"Thus, in the ripened play
Of thy perfected powers,
Thy manhood will resentments stay,
Tho' conquering what devours."

I asked: Did perfect love,
Thus all thy life posess?
It answered: "Nay, my greenness strove
In selfish bitterness.

"The inner life-divine
Did thus the basis found,
And strength afford to thus refine,
And shed my fragrance round."

41 A LESSON FROM THE THORN. S. M.

I saw a piercing thorn
Close by the rose's side,
I asked: Dost thou in opening morn
'Neath beauty's vestments hide?

In self-respecting tone
It answered: "Verily!
Not yet can beauty hold her throne
From all protection free:

"Tho' morning hath appeared
To fully opened eyes,
Through the long night our earth hath reared
Its darkened enemies:

"In blindly groping 'round,
The grasping hand would tear
Our tender roots from out the ground
Did thorns not teach them care;

"Or virtue's blinded sight,
As 'vanities,' would rend;
Or beauty-love, in wild delight,
Defeat our mission's end.

"Not til the open day
Its light sheds everywhere,
Can thorns and brambles pass away,
Or earth their presence spare."

---

42 REJOICE THE MORN APPEARS.

H. M. *Tune—Lenox.*

Rejoice! the morn appears—
Our nature's night is o'er!
Reformers quell your fears—
Your foes shall rule no more:

The light is spreading o'er the skies!
Arise! in manly courage rise!

The despots, quaking, strain
Their artful tyranny,
But freemen on them gain
As morning light we see:
The light is spreading o'er the skies!
Arise! in manly courage rise!

Old superstitions quail;
Monopoly takes fright;
They only dare assail
Deceitfully the right:
The light is spreading o'er the skies!
Arise! in manly courage rise!

The persecutors, see!
And "legal" robbers, all,
On old Hypocrisy
To shield themselves must call:
The light is spreading o'er the skies!
Arise! in manly courage rise!

Tho' mighty seems their power,
And mountainous their gains,
They tremble, quake, and cower,
As light flows o'er the plains:
Exult! it spreads o'er all the skies!
Arise! in manly courage rise!

---

43 MORNING VIEW OF DIVINE GRACE, AND OF WOES. H. M.

In morning's dawning light
Faith triumphs o'er our fears;—
Old superstition's fright
And fancies disappear:
As misty vapors break, we see
That God and Nature's grace is free.

And ever more and more,
  As nearer grows the view,
Its fullness we adore;
  Its workings ever true;
Through perfect law's evolving flow
  Constructing well a heaven below.

The "woes" which, in the mist,
  Vague terror woke within,
We see, as friends, assist
  To free from blunders—"sin:"
A rainbow spans life's clouded sky,
Proclaiming sunshine draweth nigh.

---

44 SUPERSTITION'S NIGHT IS O'ER.

H. M. *Tune—Lenox.*

Our souls begin to glow
  With morn's reflected rays,
Our opening eyes to know
  The love our earth displays:
Old superstition's night is o'er!
Its morbid dreams can vex no more!

No more our spirits strive
  God's image to efface,
But now begin to thrive,
  And grow in Nature's grace:
Old superstition's night is o'er!
Its morbid dreams can vex no more!

Distorted fancies fade;
  Ideals new evolve;
The "gods in wrath arrayed"
  To vapors all desolve:
Old superstition's night is o'er!
Its morbid dreams can vex no more!

Our loves, so long reviled
  As dark depravity,

Now, woke from impulse wild,
  Feel their divinity:
Old superstition's night is o'er!
Its morbid dreams can vex no more!

For those whose outer eyes
  The light cannot receive,
Its warming-beams supplies
  Their hampered souls relieve:
Old superstition's night is o'er!
Its morbid dreams can vex no more!

---

45 MORNING EFFORTS TO SCALE THE MOUNTAINS. H. M.

O Nature! as thy love
  Unfolds the opening day,
We seek to fully prove
  Its perfect light-display;
We strive to scale life's lofty mounts,
And bask in light's o'erflowing founts.

Tho' stumbling at the base,
  Where dark obstructions are,
We keep our earnest gaze
  Upon the Morning Star,
And, through them all, still force our way,
To sooner gain the open day.

No bruises will we heed,
  Nor timid "prudence" cry
From those who fear its lead,
  And fear their powers to try;
Tho' blundering oft, we'll persevere
Till standing where the light is clear.

46 THE DAY STAR HAS FAR ASCENDED.

11.

The Day Star has now far ascended the skies;
The light, fast increasing, reveals to our eyes,
In waking commotion, the vallies around,
And well-begun labor on life's higher ground.

Then let us not tarry to muse on our dreams,
But mount to the region of clear morning beams;
And, quaffing to fullness the free mountain air,
For life's earnest labor ourselves well prepare.

---

47 ANGEL VISITORS DISPERSE SUPERSTITIONS. 11.

Glorious scenes are transpiring around us—
The angels unite with us, lending their aid.
Errors now break which for ages have bound us;
The forces of truth all their stronghold's invade.

Long, in the mists of old error-effusions,
We saw all before us as "goblins" and gloom;
Deemed it a duty to nurse the delusions
Which shrouded in darkness and sorrow the tomb.

Nature appeared to all goodness a stranger,
Accursed by its God for the "sins" of our race;
Man, all "depraved," and his spirit in danger,
And having no claim to his God's "sovereign" grace.

Friends gone before us, tho' often returning,
Awoke but distrust, persecution, and dread;
At each return we, the truth undiscerning,
Beheld, dark and "ghostly" the realms of "the dead."

But, in the light of the opening morning,
Fogs break and we see angel friends with us here:
Loving companions, or guardians, warning
Whenever a pit-fall or danger is near.

Grand inspirations they aid in promoting,
Enlarging, exalting the life of the soul;
All superstitions full well antidoting;
Our life now is glory, and "death" is its goal.

---

48 LONGINGS FOR PERFECTED LIFE HARMONY. 11.

O Nature! I long to see body and soul
Well ripened, thy laws each in perfect control—
The germs all unfolded in harmony free
Of life unobstructed united to thee.

The visions of truth which at times greet my eyes,
The lessons of wisdom my soul then espies—
Thy provident laws, which so surely prevail,
I would not lose sight of when sorrows assail.

I would that my eyes through all clouds could but see
Thy wisdom well working in all things for me;
And ever in life's every turmoil behold
The ultimate harmony surely unfold.

The deep love fraternal that warms in my breast,
I would it should calm selfish passions to rest—
From hatred and strifes, and all sordidness free,
Toward fellows with whom I'm united in thee.

The soul-elevation of spirit inspired;
The vigor with which then my being is fired;
The hope, joy, and courage, the faith's opening sight,
I would not have checked by the darkness of night.

The conscious relation to the loving God
No more e'er obscured by the sense of the clod,
Nor my angel-sense overlook or despise
Its base in the earth when it towers to the skies.

---

49 TYRANNY COWERS BEFORE THE MORNING TOILERS. 11.

Tyranny's minions, who prowled as despoilers
Through all the long night of our infancy-years,
Start from their rioting, now, as the toilers
Arise for their rights as the morning appears.

Every leaf-rustling increases their terror;
A foe they behold in each son of the light;
With waning faith in old dogmatic error,
They strive in its name still to rally and fight.

Each dawning ray of the opening morning,
Reflected, they see as a fire in their rear.
Each uttered thought they behold as a warning
That darkness desolves, that the morning is here.

---

50 COME JOIN WITH OUR ARMY. 11.

Come join with our army, which battles to-day
That freedom and truth over man may have sway;
That greed, pride and error no more may control,
Nor old superstition e'er darken the soul.

Tho' hard is our contest, now plainly we see
The haughty foes waver, preparing to flee;
Their ardor is waning; they break and divide;
The armies of truth they can never abide.

Behold! they are weakening, and trembling with
fright;
They dare now no longer maintain open fight;
They seek all their movements to vail from our eyes,
And war by deception, in ambush-disguise.

Their banners are drooping and faint is the roar
Of all the creed-cannons, so mighty of yore;
They seek now as allies, to aid in their plight,
The forces long cursed as the "foes of the light."

They grasp "worldly" tactics and let "worldlings"
lead;
Invoke "worldly wisdom." to help them succeed;
The old creedling captains as privates appear;
While arts branded "worldly," their "piety" cheer.

Come! join with our army, and hasten the day
When truth and the right shall have fully the sway;
Help us soon to conquer the forces of wrong,
And 'neath the Truth Banner sing victory's song.

---

51 TRUTH'S CHILDREN VICTORIOUS.

11.

Children of light, now the morning is breaking,
Wide o'er the hills where the darkness has lain;
Despot-oppressors with terror are quaking—
All their vaunted powers they find on the wane.

Mists of old errors around them are thinning;
Are breaking at times to the strengthening rays,
"Demons" and "goblins," they find, are beginning
To vanish as light their true nature displays.

Despots now chiefly their purposes cover—
'Neath robes of hypocrisy shelter would find:
Each strikes at freedom in guise of a lover,
Disguised as an ally, her soldiers to blind.

See! from the robes of deceit circling 'round them,
They strive to reflect stolen rays from the morn;
Thus as the rising beams, gaining, confound them,
Pretend to work well for the cause that they scorn.

All their successes betray desperation;
Their cunning and craft are revealing their fears;
The dawning light now begins new creation;
Come! join in the work, for the morning appears.

---

52 LABORERS, THE DAY BREAKS. 11.

Children of labor, the day-dawn is breaking;
The day when old despots can plunder no more:
See! in all lands how the people are waking;
Rejoice! for the night of oppression is o'er.

Strong are their forces. but ye shall subdue them,
And scatter their legions and sweep them away:
Behold, they retreat e'er ye start to persue them!
As light falls upon them they shrink in dismay.

Children of labor, the day breaking o'er us
Shall know only justice and full liberty:
Shout! for the foe shall no more stand before us,
But all shall be brethren, in true equity.

---

53 WE BUILD NO TOY-TEMPLES. 11.

No childish toy-temples of fanciful pride
For manhood's true worshipful souls we provide;
No "sacrifice" bring we of "victims once slain;"
No souls bowed in sorrow and trembling with pain.

With heads lifted up in the day-beams, so bright,
And eyes widely opened to welcome the light,

We find every portion of infinite space
The true sanctuary—the center of grace.

We meet by the road-side, in fields, or the wood,
By sea-shore, the streamlet, or wild rushing flood,
At home or in workshop; we find everywhere
A temple of worship, an altar of prayer.

Our lives, now released from the blinding control
Of old superstition, which darkens the soul,
Exult in the wondrous creative display
Of wisdom divine which is crowding our way.

We strike hands with Nature and God, evermore,
In true labor-worship, with which we adore
The soul of all being, the fountain of life,
Whose love turns to harmony every strife.

We know that, at last, on our earth it shall give
A heaven completed to all that shall live:
The Temple Divine *they* shall see, in that day,
Who now with toy-temples that love would portray.

---

54 ENCOURAGEMENT UNDER DEFEAT.

11.

Children of light and of labor, arising
  For justice and manhood's true freedom to fight,
Banded foes, desperate, still are devising
  Dark treachery-schemes for their contests with right.

Thus, for a time, they may often defeat you,
  As, conscious of right, you reject all disguise;
They steal *your watch-words*, and craftily meet you
  As false friends, who, fawning, cast dust in your eyes.

But, in the gloomy hour, when all before you
  Grows dim till the morning rays all disappear,

Know 'tis but moving mists, just passing o'er you ;
Look sharply ! some breaks will reveal rays to cheer !

Every success of the despotic forces
But leaves them less skillful to use *their old arms.*
These fogs will break, and, their falsehood-discourses,
Reacting, will paralyze them with alarms.

Eyes of your friends, they have blinded, unclosing,
Will see their deception and join in your fight ;
The language of freedom they learned for opposing,
Will then serve to forward the triumph of right.

---

55 THE LABORERS' FOES COWERING.

11.

See, honest toilers, your foes all are cowering !
They quake as the morning sheds on them the light ;
No more, in sense of a strength overpowering,
They wage open war with the friends of the right.

Tactics of cowardice only can serve them ;—
With bribes, slurs, and slanders, your force they divide.
Spurn their regards! self-respect will unnerve them ;
Their army is wavering, while yours they divide.

Epithets aid them ; their cunning confuses
Your half-waking sense of propriety true.
Measures they slur, their self-interest uses
To gain them success in the work they persue :

Sneering at *your* thought of co-operation,
As "folly's most wild and fanatical dream,"
Corporate unions—*their* "legal" creation,
They make serve completely each plundering scheme.

Look, then, ye toilers; 'tis only clear-seeing
You need to enthrone perfect liberty here;
Strike! and, from old institutions once freeing,
Your foes will soon join you the day-dawn to cheer.
C. S. W.

---

56 RALLY, YE ARMY OF LABOR. 11.

Rally, ye army of labor, for action;
As light dawns, monopoly's legions all cower;
Rally; unite; let no spirit of faction
Deprive you of liberty, now in your power.

Charge, then, with valor, their wings and their center,
And give them no time to recover from fright;
Storm every refuge its soldiers shall enter,
Nor hold till they cease for oppression to fight.

Scan every spot where an ambush can gather;
For only when covered they venture to stand:
Forced to the light open field, they will, rather,
Throw down all their arms, and, before you, disband.

---

57 THE DAY STAR.

11, 8. *Tune—Meditation.*

We wake from our slumber, and glorious light
Flows over our long-darkened way;
We look, and the Morning-Star rises in sight;
It heralds the dawning of day.

The silvery luster of its glowing beams
Makes all lesser stars quickly pale;
It spreads o'er the earth, o'er its fields, lakes, and streams,
Descending from mountain to vale.

Earth's energies quicken, and the bounding air,
Enlivening, more freely inspires;
Increasing activity starts everywhere,
As life in its glory refires:

The songs of the birds, all awaking, we hear
In semi-tone chirpings ascend;
And manhood, long dreaming in dark morbid fear,
Begins all his fetters to rend.

Yes, this is the Day-Star! and brightly it shines
All over the long-darkened ground;
The soul's inner sense now, unfolding, refines,
Responding to light shed around.

O glorious herald of manhood's glad day,
We joy well to know that thy rays,
In soul-lighting luster, around us shall play
Till melting in sunlight's full blaze.

---

58 OPENING MORNING'S JOYOUS VIEW.

11, 8. *Tune—Meditation.*

O Morning! how joyously beam on our sight
The glories thy coming displays,
While 'round us, transforming, the "goblins" of night
Enrobe in the bright shining rays.

Our pathway of life we now find is replete
With Nature's abounding supplies;
No "pitfalls of error" now "yawn at our feet"—
The mists, that distorted, arise.

The "tempters," which "crowded to lead us astray,"
We find were our nature's true friends—
The angels of love, who were pointing the way
For the vigor which nature defends.

The "frowns" which appeared on the Visage-Divine,
We find were the smilings of grace;
The "flashes of wrath" were the glories that shine
In love, which illumines his face.

The earth is revealed to our wondering sight,—
A primary school of kind heaven;
Where bliss, in a slowly unfolding delight,
To man's cultured nature is given.

O gropers in darkness, now open your eyes,
And mount to the regions of day!—
The highlands are glowing with sunbeam-supplies,
And all of their glory-display.

---

59 HOW TO AWAKEN THE SLEEPERS.

11, 8. *Tune—Meditation.*

O brothers who joy in the morning's glad beams,
Let us in true vigor arise,
And work for our fellows who, struggling in dreams,
Would hold to the darkness which flies.

They strive in a horror that curdles their blood,
Yet hug their delusion and fear;
But each struggling streamlet of the vital flood
Half feels that the morning is near.

They see us as foes when in kindness we call,
And bid them awake to the day;
The bright scintillations, around them, appall;
Distorted, they fill with dismay.

Thus dark persecutions they call to their aid,
That they in the fog may remain;
Each rallying effort of friends seems a raid
Of "demons," to plunge them in pain.

The mists of the morning make lurid the glow
  Of each morning ray playing 'round—
Makes kind love fraternal, "malignity's flow,
  To plunge them in sorrow profound."

But tho' waking struggles, commingling with dreams,
  Against us their efforts employ,
Let us, all uniting, let in the day-beams,
  And we shall awake them to joy.

---

60 THE JUDGMENT MORNING COMES.

8, 7.

Lo, it comes, the long-expected
  Judgment morning of our earth,
When our reason-germ, perfected,
  Shall at last have gained its birth.
Long its labor-throes have given
  Painful "creeds," to rack the soul;
Now the dawn spreads o'er the heaven,
  Vital energies control.

Every eye, with joy surprising,
  Soon shall open to the light;
Every soul, new-born, arising,
  Drop the vestures of the night.
Breathing then the inspiration
  Of the newly-quickened air,
They shall soon, in transformation,
  Grow to manhood everywhere.

Faith, well grounded and maturing,
  Shall behold, with manly eye,
Heaven-foundations here, enduring,
  Linking with the heavens on high:—
Clearly, through the mists dissolving,
  Man his "Saviour" here shall see—

Wisdom—in his life evolving,
  Which from blunders "sin" shall free.

Shout! ye first-born of the morning,
  Who have gained the highland view,
And beheld the earth adorning
  In the light unclouded, true;
Sunlight shall in greater glory
  Through the earth unfold the day.
Sound aloud the gospel story
  Of the light's all-conquering sway!

---

61 MORNING MOVEMENTS. 8, 7.

Look! the light is o'er us breaking;
  Morning gleams illume the skies;
All the mists are in commotion;
  See! they break before our eyes.
List! the chirping notes of gladness
  Birds of morn begin to sing.
Let their strains dispel all sadness;
  See! they venture on the wing.

Science, rising from her slumbers
  And the truth-distorting dreams,
Dimly seeing, crudely blunders,
  Then begins to catch the beams:
Classifying, in position
  Facts arrange, revealing cause;
Opening, to our erudition,
  Knowledge of great Nature's laws.

Fogs grow thinner; eyes grow stronger;—
  Nature's God by man is seen;—
Superstition can no longer
  Fully hold its mists between:
Manhood wakes to its condition,
  Challenges its kingly foes;

Woman claims her true position,
  Spurns whatever dares oppose

"Moral" dogmas, persecution,
  Tyrant-greed, monopoly,
Now, foreboding dissolution,
  To the thickest vapors fly.
Cheer! ye struggling prophet-toilers–
  Champions of the truth and right,
Ye shall conquer all despoilers!
  Now appears the morning light!

---

62 MORNING INSPIRATIONS. 8, 7.

All around us, notes of gladness
  Fall upon the listening ear,
And the tones of shrinking sadness
  Lessen as the day draws near:
E'en the morbid dreamers, quaking
  In a superstition-fright,
From their fancies half-awaking,
  Catch some gleams of morning light.

Often those whose *outer* senses
  Are in dozing-stupor still,
Find their *inner*, gain defenses,
  Strengthening reason, thought, and will,
While the Saving Light they're dreading,
  As a "soul-destroying fire,"
Evermore, around them spreading,
  Much their souls it doth inspire.

Faith now holds its earth-foundations
  When it strives to mount the skies;
Less it flutters in gyrations—
  With more steady wing it flies.
Ever wider are its ranges;
  Higher, higher still it soars;
Less the fog the view deranges
  When the life-field it explores.

And, while half-awaking vision
  Larger inspiration feels,
Senses open find elysian,
  Here, the morning light reveals:
Finds the heaven to earth united,
  Angels bringing us its cheer;
Faith, becoming clear, all-sighted,
  Finds perfecting-law is here.

---

63 HASTEN, MORNING. 8, 7.

Hasten on, thou coming morning!
  All our souls of thee have need;
Let thy rays, our earth adorning,
  Quicken manly life and deed;
Faith refiring and inspiring—
  Faith that blossoms bearing seed,
Till aspiring souls, desiring
  Real gospel, here may feed.

Earnest natures darkly labor
  To promote our human weal
By denying self and neighbor
  Truths that morning rays reveal;
Giving ever their endeavor,
  With intensest bigot-zeal
Made a lever, hearts to sever
  From the love divine they feel.

Superstition-mists, around them,
  So distort their spirits' view
That the morning rays confound them,
  Till the false appears the true:
Till they're praying that decaying
  Faith may crush the live and new;
Truth obeying, deeming "straying;"
  "Sinful" all that truth persue.

Let thy glory-beams, increasing,
  Soon their blinding mists remove,

Till, distortions wholly ceasing,
  Light shall reach their dogma-grove;
Love clear-sighted, truly lighted,
  Their ideals will improve;
And, benighted fancy righted,
  Piety the light will love.

Then, in fullness of the blessing
  Which the open light shall give,
Every soul, in love progressing,
  Shall for real welfare live.
Then each being, clearly seeing
  Whence the blessings that relieve,
Shall, in freeing light agreeing,
  Real aid from all receive.

---

64 DAY-BEAMS WARM BODY AND SOUL.

8, 7.

Morning light, now flowing o'er us,
  Warms anew our vital blood,
While the opening view, before us,
  Cheers the newly-quickened flood.
Long, in half-stagnation courses,
  It has struggled through each vein,
Striving 'gainst malarial forces,
  Which had poisoned heart and brain:

Dreams of "wrath" and "condemnation,"
  Broke our rest in sleeping hours;
Rheums and agues racked sensation
  In our half-awaking powers:
Struggling faith, tho' ever seeking
  To maintain its active sway,
Gave but superstitions, reeking
  With miasmas' foulest play.

All ideals gave distorted
  Shapes unto the spirit's view,

Which, as error, greatly thwarted
  Efforts for the good and true;
God and Nature's loving features
  Seemed to frown with selfish wrath,
Sending curses on their "creatures,"
  Scattering woes upon their path.

Man was seen, "A feeble being
  By great tempters made to fall;
All depraved, no power for freeing
  From the snares which souls enthrall."
Angel friends, when circling round us,
  Seemed but "demons" "to ensnare;"
Lurking foes, who would confound us,
  Seemed besetting everywhere.

But the dawning, breaking o'er us,
  Warm anew our vital blood,
While the opening view, before us,
  Cheers the newly-quickened flood:
Life and health, from love and beauty,
  Warm the body, heart and soul;
Grandest pleasures blend with duty
  As the day-beams o'er us roll.

---

65 SEE, YE FEARFUL! YOUR PATH BRIGHTENS. 8, 7.

Day is dawning; see! ye toiling
  Strugglers through our nature's night,
Who, in partial life-awaking,
  Stumble forward, seeking light—
Ye whose intuitions, rousing
  From old superstition-dreams,
Strive to pioneer your progress,
  See! the morning round you beams.

Look! and soon, with clearer vision,
  You will see your life prevails

Over every seeming "evil
  Which its vital power assails;"
That its pains are only transient
  Monitorial promptings, true,
Pointing out the path of pleasure
  You are seeking to pursue.

See! less dismal grows your pathway!
  Seeming pitfalls, "threatening harm,"
Prove but shallow, marshy spaces,
  Which should never cause alarm:
E'en the vale of "death," before you,
  Dark and fearful seems no more—
There you see no "vengeful flashes,"
  Such as vexed your souls of yore.

Steadfast, look! and, as the daybeams
  Break the mists before your eyes,
You will see, beyond the valley,
  The celestial mountains rise;
That "the death-fiend" is an angel
  Leading to a brighter day,
With a hand of love extended,
  While the other points the way.

---

66 MORNING LIGHT BRINGS A GOSPEL.

8, 7.

Long the gloomy night has lingered,
  And the mists o'erspread the sky,
Till no ray but feeble starlight
  Dimmed by vapors met the eye;
Or when mists were partly breaking,
  As by surging tempests torn,
Came but fitful and distorted,
  Leaving us the more forlorn.

But the morning light is dawning;
  Deeper grows the spreading gray;

All the mists are in commotion,
  Thinning in the breaking day:
Clearer, clearer now, before us,
  Nature opens to our view;
Ever the distortions straighten,
  And ideals shape anew:

All the horrid fancies, cherished
  As eternal truth, divine,
Are dissolving, reconstructing,
As the day-beams 'round them shine:
Man is seen, the child, well cherished
  By Almighty Power and Love;
"Woes," but monitors, to teach him
  Pleasure's path if he should rove.

Morning light thus brings a gospel
  To the hungry, famished soul,
Satisfying nature's cravings;
  This can make the wounded whole!
Send its message to all nations,
  Till each needy soul shall see
Nature's all-supplying fountain,
  Ever open, ever free.

---

67 MORNING BRINGS NEW CREATION.

8, 7.

Now we see, with joy nd gladness,
  Manhood's dawning morning-light
Scattering all the misty sadness
  Of old superstition's night.
This is heaven's divinest treasure;
  Every blessing with it blends
In an all-supplying measure,
  And upon our earth descends.

This unfolds a new creation,
  Working 'round us every hour;

Earthly scenes, in transformation,
  Glow with heavenly life and power.
Man, awaking, starts to action,
  Shares the flowing morning-gleams;
And, unheeding creed or faction,
  Scales the mounts for fuller beams.

There no saddened tones of pleading
  Load the breath of manly prayer:
Man, his life's own promptings heeding,
  Working, grasps his answer there.
Let us, all obstructions spurning,
  Toward the summits force our way,
From ou purrpose never turning
  Till we bask in open day.

MORNING LIGHT WILL GIVE US HEAVEN. 8, 7.

Joyously our souls awaken,
  As our manhood-morning's hour
Sheds its dawning rays around us,
  In their all-illuming power:
Views sublime unfold before us
  As the vapors roll away,
And the day-beams, ever clearing,
  Nature's opening fields display

All the half-seen glory-glimpses
  Of Ideal's early dreams
Were, we see, but dim reflections
  Of our morning's rising beams:
Ever, as the light increases,
  Larger, grander still, they grow,
Then, as newer rise, are fading
  In the daylight's freer flow.

Grandest flight of poet's fancy
  Scarcely can its thought express

Ere the opening light, so real,
  Dims the luster of the dress.
Soon, in fully-open morning,
  Truth undimmed shall all receive;
And the perfect light, transforming,
  Heaven complete to earth shall give.

---

69 HEAVEN'S BUILDING-LAW WORKING HERE. 8, 7.

In the morning breaking o'er us,
  While but twilight meets our eyes,
All the opening view before us
  Gives us cheering soul-surprise:
Earth is seen with beauty glowing,
  Well unfolding heavenly love,
On each open heart bestowing
  Foretaste of the heaven above.

All the "evils," so distressing,
  Now we see are but the sway
Of the forming-laws, progressing
  While obstructions block their way:
"Poisons," misplaced building forces,
  Or dross-solvents misapplied,
"Death" but nature's law divorces
  'Twixt the lives no more allied;

Pain, the faithful guardian angel
  Of the soul's unfolding form;
Prompting wisdom—life's evangel,
  Till it learns to check the storm;
Earthquakes, spreading desolation,
  Tempests, dark contagion-woe,
But life-force in inflammation
  Its obstructions to o'erthrow.

And we see that passions breaking
  Forth into excesses wild,

Are but trammel-burstings, making
  Room for Nature's growing child:
See Ideal's blindest blunder,
  In its thought of moral law,
Cannot keep our nature under—
  That its bands will prove as straw.

Yes, we see, the "great destroyer,"
  Laying joy and virtue low,
Is the Life-Divine employer,
  Bidding builders forward go:
'Hells" the discord of the clearing
  Grounds for heaven arising here.
Yes! we see the city rearing,
  As the light is growing clear.

---

70 MY SOUL'S JOY IN THE LIGHT. 8, 7.

Dogma-darkness, now forever
  Thou hast left my tortured soul!
Thy old chilling gloom can never
  More my manly powers control!
Tho' by thee so long surrounded,
  I have risen to see the light;
Reason is no more confounded
  By forebodings and affright.

Now, serenely here abiding,
  Peace and joy my nature fills;
From my God no more I'm hiding;
  I delight in what he wills:
"Sins," I see, but blunders; saviours
  All the pains they bring to teach;
"Death" the pioneer, whose favor
  Makes all life to serve for each.

And, I see, tho' many, dreary,
  In the darkening mists abide,

Starving for the truth, and weary
  For the rest they spurn and chide,
"Sins," and pains, and "death" are serving
  Cherished errors to dissolve,
While their souls, so well deserving,
  In great Nature's grace evolve.

---

71 THE WAKING CRY. 8, 7.

Wake, O man! the Day-Star rises!
  See! He mounts the glowing sky;
Now his lighting beams are flowing
  On each fully-opened eye;
Wake! Behold! and then, rejoicing,
  Thou wilt join the waking cry,
And, thy nature's life adoring,
  Know thy nature's God is nigh.

Wake! ye who, in troubled sleeping,
  Struggle with your morbid dreams,
"Goblin" forms are disappearing—
  Morning through your lattice gleams;
Wake! your fancied "flames of vengeance"
  Are the light's caressing beams;
Wake! Behold! their fond, endearing
  Love flows 'round you, now, in streams.

Wake to life of manly action!
  To its fruits of manly joy!
Wake! and Nature's truths and beauties
  Will your manly powers employ,
And the superstition-terrors
  Will no more their work destroy;
Wake! and joys shall blend with duties,
  Joys which fear cannot alloy.

72 WAKE FROM SUPERSTITION. 8, 7.

Lift your eyes, ye long-benighted!
  Wake from superstition-fear;
See! the earth around is lighted;
  See! the dawn of day is here;
See! the mists are in commotion;
  Wake from morbid-dream affright!
Rise from morbid, fear devotion!
  Rise and greet the morning light!

Wake to manly life-endeavor;
  Let your widely-opened eyes
See that Nature's laws, forever,
  Give us perfect life-supplies:
See! The "evils," which alarm you,
  Ever teach the laws of joy,
That your blunders may not harm you
  When your powers find true employ.

See! as blinding mists are thinning,
  Fancied "demons" prove your friends,
And your "penalty" for "sinning"
  But the work which folly mends.
Nature's God, with smiling features,
  Greets you in the dawning day;
Never frowns upon his "creatures,"
  Never casts his wards away.

---

73 ASCEND THE HIGHLANDS. 8, 7.

Brothers, who are vainly trying,
  In the lingering mists, to find
Inspirations well supplying
  The aspiring human mind,
See! the morning-dawn is breaking!
  See! the mountains tower before!
Scale their hights, the fogs forsaking—
  Nature's open fields explore.

Mount where vapors are dispersing;
Where the soul, with open eyes,
Can, with nature's God conversing,
Find unfailing life-supplies.
Leave traditions, dim and dying,
And their fetid atmosphere
Here are highland fields, supplying
Vital currents fresh and clear.

Hasten where the light is flowing
Undistorted all around,
Where the wholesome plants are growing
Over all the gladdened ground;
Seek no more your life to nourish
On the fungus of decay;
Living shoots abundant flourish,
Which would give it healthy play.

Here the fields already whiten
With the promised fruit-supply;
Fragrant blossoms hourly brighten,
Yield perfume and cheer the eye.
Mount the highlands, never turning
Once a lingering look behind!
All your nature's life is yearning
For supplies you here may find.

---

74 THE CHARGE TO NATURE'S FREE-MEN. 8, 7.

Nature's freemen, take your stations!
Be the leaders in the van
Of our earth's advancing nations,
Of your struggling fellow-man,
Blindly striving, ever striving
Nature's law of life to scan—
Their evolving life-creation—
Love Divine's unfolding plan.

Bid the darkened, dogma preachers—
"Blinded leaders of the blind,"
Stand aside for Nature's teachers,
Take their stations, now, behind.
Help their victims, struggling victims,
From the "ditch" their way to find,
And remove from spirit-features
That which darkens thus the mind.

Take your stations, tho' excited
Priestly despots loudly rail;
Show the pious souls benighted,
Nature ever will prevail—
True religion—free religion,
Will old dogma-power impale;
Pausing not till, earth well lighted,
"Creeds" no more can truth assail

Let the priestly pride no longer
You as "worldlings" classify!
True religion will be stronger
When it works with open eye;
Well assert it! now assert it!
Error's haughty hosts will fly;
Then, well known, none e'er shall wrong her,
From her light none hide the eye.

---

75 MORNING PROPHETS, YOUR WORK PREVAILS 8, 7.

Prophets of the dawning morning,
See! as light increases 'round,
Those who met your call with scorning
Now begin to scan the ground:
While *your* upward view ignoring,
They, with clearing earth-bound eyes,
Life's foundations are exploring,
For the structure soon to rise.

Science delves in brave endeavor
  To well base philosophy;
And her blows well serve to sever
  Ruins which around her lie.
Many, while by vapors darkened,
  Feel the warming morning-rays,
And unconsciously have harkened
  To the truth the light displays.

In the priestly institutions
  Social life and arts revive;
"Creeds" are kept in thin dilutions,
  For the weakly sensitive:
The ecclesiastic preachers
  Lean on old Hypocrisy;
Morning prophets, you're the teachers!
  See! old superstitions die!

---

76 ANGEL FRIENDS WITH US. 8, 7.

Now, as dawn is deepening o'er us,
  We behold, around us stand,
Loving friends who've gone before us
  To the joyous angel land:
When the heart is deeply yearning
  For the tender soul-caress,
From their heaven they, oft returning,
  Find it heaven our lives to bless.

Angel friends, no more our lonely
  Longing hearts, in slavish fear,
Spurn your converse, thinking "only
  'Demon foes' surround us here:"
Morning rays, around us streaming,
  The distorting mists remove,
Till no more your smiles are seeming
  "Frowns, to blight our life and love."

Joys unknown our souls are warming,
  For, before our wondering eyes,

"Goblin-forms" are all transforming,
Heaven we see on earth arise:
No forebodings dark, of sorrow,
Golden memories alloy;
Now we know' a heavenly morrow
Fully shall unfold our joy.

---

77 ANGELS, OUR MORNING VISITORS.

8, 7.

Lo! in morning's dawning glory,
While our hearts expand with cheer,
And old errors, worn and hoary,
In the light soon disappear,
Angels join us, freely join us,
In our social circles here,
Tinting earth with rainbow-glory
From the higher heavenly sphere.

Mists all melt, no more distorting,
Angels as our friends are known:
From fraternal love resorting
To the scenes which were their own,
Giving gladness, buoyant gladness,
Giving hope its rightful throne,
Strengthening it till, fears all thwarting,
None in sadness e'er shall moan.

Now we see, their ministrations
Are through God and Nature's law,
As in all the love-relations
Kindred souls together draw.
This is perfect, fully perfect,
With no lacking and no flaw,
All-sufficient for "salvation:"
Ills before it are as straw.

"Goblin" dreams and terrors vanish;—
God and angels, with us here,

Lighten care, distortions banish,
  Make our "woes" our pathway clear
For our progress, onward progress,
  Toward a perfect heavenly sphere.
This when love is ripe, unclannish,
  We shall see on earth appear.

---

78 PARTING INVOCATION FOR MORNING WORKERS. 8, 7.

Now, in parting, may the blessing
  Of the light's unceasing flow,
Evermore our souls possessing,
  Mould our lives where'er we go,
And inspire us, well inspire us,
  Real duty well to know;
That to fields of truest labor
  We our efforts may bestow.

May no prejudices blind us;
  May the light of dawning day
Cast the lingering mists behind us,
  And illumine well our way,
Till the glowing, warming, glowing
  Sunbeams there, may so display
The inviting path of progress,
  That no footsteps e'er can stray.

Till this joyous consummation
  Let our diligence and care
Freely join in earnest labor
  With our fellows everywhere;
And remember, well remember,
  Each our neighbor's toil to share,
Till, in light, the race all workers,
  Joyous work the *toil* shall spare.

79 THE WATCHMAN'S MORNING TRUMPET. 8, 7. 6 l.

Hark! the watchman's trumpet, sounding,
  Now proclaims the dawn of day—
Manhood's day, when truth, abounding,
  Finds a larger, freer play.
Send the tidings to all nations—
  Tidings of the dawning day.

Science wakes from dreamy slumbers,
  Finds the universal laws;
Poesy exalts its numbers—
  Shows the All-Relating Cause.
Spread the light through every nation;
  Show them Nature's work and cause.

Inspiration learns its mission,
  And its universal play;
Science, raised to true condition,
  Joins it; leads it on the way.
Let it soon, its laws revealing,
  Lead from error's darkened way.

Superstition's trembling legions
  Seek the thickest mists in vain;
For the light has pierced the regions
  Of the fog-invested plain.
Send the light till, fogs dissolving,
  It shall deluge all the plain.

---

80 MANHOOD'S DAY IS DRAWING NIGH.

8, 7. 6 l.

Freedom toilers, lo the morning
  Beams o'er all the Eastern sky!
See! the light, the hills adorning,
  To the valleys draweth nigh.

Mark the tokens! much betokens
  Manhood's day is drawing nigh.

On the hills the birds are singing;
  Listen! hear their tuneful lays!
Every zephyr-breath is bringing
  Notes their joyous voices raise.
Mark the tokens! cheering tokens
  Of the sunlight's coming rays.

Despots start in wild commotion,
  Struggling, in despairing plight,
To make ignorant devotion
  Serve to bar the morning light.
Mark the tokens! stirring tokens!
  Right begins to show its might.

Kingly craft and priests', conspiring,
  Newer subterfuges try;
But the people's hearts are firing,
  Manhood's day is drawing nigh.
Mark the tokens! *all* betokens
  Manhood's day is drawing nigh.

---

81 RALLYING CALL TO THE NEW BUILDERS. 8, 7. 6 l.

Dogma's night and desolation
  Long upon our earth has lain,
But there comes a new creation—
  Morning dawns o'er hill and plain;
And the chilled and nearly blighted
  Plants revive with life again.

Ruined wrecks of former ages
  Lie in fragments strown around;
And their builders' wrath enrages
  When we strive to clear the ground;
But we know 'tis manly duty
  Needed structures new to found.

Let us, then, be up and doing,
  All who, waking, see the light;
Ever active, well pursuing
  The demands of truth and right;
There is nothing that opposes
  But the love-inverting blight.

---

82 DESPOTS' ARTS IN FREEDOM'S MORNING. 8, 7. 6 l.

Freedom's morning now is nearing;
  See! o'er all the Eastern sky,
How the deepening gray, appearing,
  Makes the mists and darkness fly;
How the despots, troubled despots,
  Quaking, newer arts must try!

Thrones appeal unto the people
  As their source of "rights divine;"
The cathedral-tower and steeple
  For the "worldly" friendships pine;
And their builders, crafty builders,
  "Worldly" skill with "faith" combine.

"Worldly" rulers, most despising
  All ecclesiastic power,
Seek to kill, yet, succor prising,
  Streams of flattery on it shower;
Priests all cowering, inly cowering,
  Laud the "laws" they would devour.

Despotism now decomposes—
  Each lone element, in strife,
'Neath Hypocrisy opposes
  Secretly the others' life.
Theirs is but desolving vigor,
  Where but treachery is rife:

War must wait till Greed has voted;
  Greed to thought must bow the knee;

Bigotry must seem devoted
  To all liberality.
Prophet toilers, freedom toilers,
  You may here your triumph see!

---

83 MANHOOD'S DAY DAWNS. 8, 7.

Manhood's day at length is breaking!
  Through the mists it sheds its rays!
Eyes which seek the truth, awaking,
  Find it opening to their gaze.

Active souls who scale the mountains,
  Where the view is open, clear,
See the sunlight's flowing fountains,
  And the morning star appear.

Wake! arouse! ye long-discouraged,
  Dozing champions of the right;
Wake to action; well encouraged;
  Strike for manhood, in the light.

Despot foes, in darkness hoarding,
  Deem ye conquered, sleep secure;
Wake! the light is now affording
  Victory that will endure.

---

84 THE JUDGMENT TRUMPET. 8, 7.

God the token-word hath spoken—
  Science gives the "trumpet-sound;
"Creeds" all broken, well betoken
  Mighty changes all around.

Errors, fearing, partly hearing,
  Shrink at Nature's judgment-blast;
As appearing, ever nearing,
  Her archangel comes at last.

Now the sounding trump, resounding,
  Wakes from dogma-graves their dead;
While surrounding light, confounding,
  Dazzling, plays around each head.

As ascending souls are blending
  With the truth-illumined sky,
Error's bending power is ending;
  False authority must fly.

Institutions, in dilutions
  Fashion "creeds," to hold their sway;
'Mid confusions, old illusions
  They behold all pass away.

The consuming fires, illuming
  The new earth, the old destroy;
Truths now blooming, sway assuming,
  More and more our powers employ.

---

85 NATURE'S GOD TO MAN HAS SPOKEN.

8, 7.

Nature's God to man has spoken!
  By his voice, in every land,
Persecution's power is broken—
  Undisguised it cannot stand.

Now its hand and shriveling fingers
  Wield no more the sword of power;
In disguise it merely lingers,
  Growing feebler every hour:

Priestly chains, by rust of ages,
  Cankered, rotted, hold no more;
Nature opens wide her pages;
  Seers abound as ne'er before.

By Hypocrisy protected,
  Propped by power of reigning Greed,

Dogma's bulwarks, best erected,
Crumbling, serve no more its need.

Nature's living shoots are springing
Forth to life o'er all the ground;
Chimes of science-truths are ringing;
Her foundation-laws are found.

Nature's God to man has spoken;
Where his voice is clearly heard
Superstition-faiths are broken
'Neath his nature-written word.

Pass the word to error's forces!
When the people understand,
Heeding Nature's wise discourses,
Error's armies must disband.

---

86 DESPOTISM BEGINS ITS ENDING. 8, 7.

Soldier for the right contending,
Let thy courage never fail!
Despotism begins its ending,
Freedom's forces will prevail.

Tho' the battle rages 'round thee,
'Tis the foes' despairing charge;
They can never more confound thee,
Tho' their numbers may be large.

See! their energy is wasting—
Coward-arts—deceit they try;
Thou art ever on them gaining;
Soon their haughty hosts will fly.

Onward! see! their ammunition,
(Failing fast, and blindly used)
Oft rebounding, their position
Sweeping, has their ranks confused:

While with freedom's forces striving,
Freedom's battle-cry they sound—
"Justice!" "law!" their shouts reviving
Freedom-inspiration 'round.

Fears o'erwhelm them, paralyzing
All their ever-vaunted powers;
Now, in manly strength arising,
Strike! the day will soon be ours.

---

87 DESPOTISM'S COWARDLY TACTICS.

8, 7.

Brothers, let no thought of sadness
Faith and joyous hope confound,
When old dspotism, in madness,
Strikes your fellows to the ground.

Tho' the friends of truth assailing,
Often seeming to succeed,
Closely scan it! when prevailing,
All its tactics weakness plead.

By its craft in false pretenses,
Now, from victims, it must gain
Prejudice for its defenses,
Or its efforts prove in vain:

"Moral purity's protection,"
To the blinded crowd it cries;
From their rights gains their defection
But by dust cast in their eyes.

---

88 NATURE'S EVOLUTION-PROMISE. 8, 7.

Hear ye not the golden promise,
Nature to her children gives?

"My constructing-hand shall finish
  To perfection all that lives:

"I will make the dreaded 'evil,'
  Dreary shadow pass away;
And, from darkness soon evolving,
  Thou shalt see the beaming day.

"Lower forms and lower forces
  Shall foundations lay for man;
Who, in fullest life-unfolding,
  The causation-laws shall span.

"Thus thy childish hopes, tho' 'failing,'
  Will give larger life-supply;
Not a throe is unavailing,
  Not a tear in sorrow's eye."

---

89 FAREWELL TO THE RISEN SOUL. 8, 7.

Risen soul, no more surrounding
  Earthly floods and billows roar;
Angel life, with joy abounding,
  Greets thee on the heavenly shore.

There thy nature's ripening glory—
  All thy loves' unfolding flow,
Free from trammels grim and hoary,
  Perfect heavenly joy shall know.

'Mid those truer life-relations,
  Well completed will appear
All that spirit-aspirations,
  Stumbling, oft predicted here.

In imperfect life-endeavor,
  We awhile must here remain;
But the soul ascendeth ever;—
  We shall meet thee soon again.

90 ANGEL FRIENDS' GREETING VOICES.

8, 7.

Hark ! what sounds are floating o'er us,
In a lively, joyous strain !—
Loving friends who've gone before us,
Come to greet us here again.

Listen ! their exulting voices
Reach us on each passing breath ;
Earth with heaven to-day rejoices.
For a friend we find in death.

Hear them cheer the new arrival !
Open reason's listening ears !
Hear our friend, in life-survival,
Triumph o'er old earthly fears !

Now our misty, morbid terrors
Change to joys in morning light ;—
Heaven and earth, through fading errors,
Join their hands within our sight.

---

91 ANGEL-CONVERSE, AND MESSAGES.

8, 7.

Hark ! while morning-life rejoices,
While awaking nature sings,
Angels add their cheering voices,
Earth with spirit-greeting rings :

Many, long esteemed as " lost ones,
Torn by 'cruel death' away,"
Say to us, the tempest-tost ones,
They are still with us to-day :

Tell us, " life is one eternal
Onward-flowing, perfect stream—
Earthly blending with supernal—
Sharing its effulgent beam :"

Tell us "death is but resigning
To the earth the outworn clay;
E'en as vital powers, refining,
Yield some portion every day;"

That "the ripe, or hampered spirit
Casts obstructing flesh aside,
Yet its earthly friends are near it,
Finding it a friend and guide."

Shout! the goblin-dreams have vanished!
Earth and heaven unite to-day;
Superstition-fears are banished:
"Hells" dissolve in morning's ray.

---

92 DAWNING MORNING.

8, 7. *Tune—Shining Shore.*

We'll join our hands, with lively cheer,
In earnest life-endeavor;
The chills of fear all disappear;
They leave us now forever.

CHORUS.—For, oh! we see the jubilee
Of manhood's dawning morning,
And earth below begin to glow—
In heavenly robes adorning.

We'll shrink no more, with tearful eyes,
From any passing sorrow;
If storms arise, the clearing skies
Will brightness from them borrow.

Let passion sweep in tempests wild!
This truth the light discloses—
Life's angel, mild, thus aids her child
'Gainst what his life opposes.

We joy in the resistless flow
Of vital inspirations;
The whirlwinds blow clears earth below,
For heavenly life's foundations.

We joy in every grand display
  Of heaven's unfolding treasure,
Which morning shows around us flows
  In soul-supplying measure.

  Cho.—For, oh! we see, etc.

---

93 ANGELS HERE.

8, 7.—*Tune—Shining Shore.*

The light is spreading o'er the sky,
  Each moment growing stronger;
Distorting mists now break and fly:
  They blind our eyes no longer.

Chorus.—For, oh! the streams of morning beams
    The plains are flowing over;
  And with us here, in social cheer,
    The angels we discover.

The loving friends who've gone before,
  We find are with us ever;
With heavenly vigor evermore
  Inspiring life-endeavor.

We see that "Death" is Life's true friend,
  Who opens wide the portal
Through which, to higher spheres, ascend
  The souls that drop the mortal:

That dying forms, in changing states,
  The life-forms are evolving:
That Nature ever thus "creates"
  From lower forms dissolving:

That, through the mighty realms of space,
  Life-pulses all are beating
Response to the nutritious grace
  "Death" yields for life-completing.

We'll join our hands, in earnest zeal,
  With angels, in erecting

A heaven below, which will reveal
The higher heavens, connecting.

CHO.—For, oh! the streams, etc.

---

94 FAITH'S MORNING ACHIEVEMENT.

8, 7, 4.

Through the vapors, earth surrounding,
Rays of dawning find their way;
Fancies crude, so long confounding,
Melt before the dawn of day:
See! the day-beams
More and more around us play.

Long we strove, in half-awaking
Struggles, to unclose our eyes,
Saw, with nightmare terror quaking,
"Demon" forms around us rise:
Deeming angels
"Fiends," who joy would sacrifice.

Thus, with frantic efforts, hiding
From imagined dangers near,
Vapor "creeds" we were providing,
As the covers for our fear,
Till the thinning
Fogs began to break and clear.

Then we roused, and, 'mid confusing,
Strange distortions all around,
Manhood powers first feebly using,
Stumbling, gained the higher ground,
Till the clearer
Morning light at length we found.

Here we find complete salvation
In our lives' unfolding play;
And we call to every nation,
Scale mounts and meet the day;
Then, enlightened,
Faith shall lead in Nature's way.

MORNING LIGHT FREES AND SAVES US. 8, 7, 4.

Morning light, increasing round us,
E'er the fogs have passed away,
Melts the icy chain that bound us,
Gives our natures freer play,
And our life-streams
Greater vigor day by day

Intuition's opening vision
Sees, in grand unfolding views,
Earth preparing fields elysian,
Decking in the heavenly hues;
Love fraternal,
Thrilling, spreads the joyful news.

Faith now finds her true foundation
In the all-sustaining laws;
There, unmoved, she grasps creation,
And the all-unfolding cause;
Which, evolving,
Well repaires the transient flaws.

Earth now shows us love eternal;
Storms its equilibrium flow;
Through the storm-cloud, joy supernal
Sheds its gleams on every woe,
Giving glimpses
Of unfolding heaven below.

Thus illumed, we see that vices—
Passion-tempests—but remove
Air befoulments and the ices
Frigid "morals" cast on love;—
"Hells" thus aid us
While we link with heaven above.

Oh! the wonderful salvation
Which our Morning brings to view!
This is real consolation,
Grace divine, almighty, true,
Free, unceasing,
Old as time, yet ever new!

Let it now, our souls expanding,
  Energise each manly power,
Till, while yet on earth we're standing,
  To the highest heavens we tower,
    And reach downward
  Loving hands the "hells" to scour.

---

96 THE SEERS' DUTY TO SLEEPING FELLOWS. 8, 7, 4.

Nature's seers, who scale the mountains,
  And discern the morning beams,
In your joyous exultation
  O'er the upward-spreading gleams,
    Still remember
  Those who strive in morbid dreams:

Just beneath you, in the vallies,
  Lingering fogs obscure the day,
Stupefying manly powers,
  Which would wake to manly play;—
    There your fellows
  Life-streams stagnate and decay.

Wildly striving to awaken
  From their superstition-fright,
Their half-opened, feeble senses
  See you as the foes of light;
    And would brand you
  "Helpers of the 'fiends' of night."

Governments, of states and churches,
  Led by greed, around them stand—
"Menial" servants—executing,
  Where they can, each wild command
    Of the blinded
  Dark resentments of the band.

Yet, unfearing, draw ye near them;
  Cry aloud, "'Tis dawning day!"

Meet with love their drowsy curses;
  Keep their roaring bulls at bay,
    Till their waking
  Powers arouse to healthy play.

---

97 HELP THE DOGMA-DARKENED.

8, 7, 4.

On the realms of dogma-darkness,
  Sons of light, in pity gaze;
See the crowds of human brothers
  Lost in superstition's maze,
    Vapors spreading
  Over all their thoughts and ways:

Dwarfed and chilled by priestly teachings
  In their tender childhood years,
Reason's vision dimmed, distorted,
  By a morbid fancy's fears,
    Error, danger,
  Nature's truth to them appears;

Reason's voice, within them speaking,
  Nature's loves, when they impel,
Are contemned and scorned, resisted,
  Deemed the "whisperings from hell."
    And benighted
  Virtue loves in chains to dwell;

Faith's intensest life-endeavor
  Closes inspiration's eyes;
Love fraternal, when controlling,
  To befog its fellows tries;
    Blinding vapors
  Deems the light to make them wise.

Sons of light, behold with pity—
  Loving pity—not with scorn!
Work with earnest zeal to rescue
  All your fellows thus forlorn;
    Help to scatter
  Fogs that vail our reason's morn.

98 GOD WITH US HERE. 7.

Morning light, in joy we see
How thy power the soul can free;
How the mists before thee flies,
Opening the effulgent skies!
Ever on resistless flow;
Change to joy our human woe;
To the souls oppressed with fear,
Show their nature's God is here.

While the daybeams dawn around,
Many still, in dread profound,
Deem them only "lures to woes,
From malignant 'demon foes;"
Thus they plunge into the mist,
And their needed light resist.
Show the timid souls sincere,
Thou, their God, art with them here.

While, in superstition-fright,
They attempt to bar the light,
And their waning faith would stay
On a "God that's far away;"
In an agonizing prayer
Calling for his aid and care,
Show his presence ever near—
Show their loving God is here.

Show them strifes of darkened years,
Pains and sorrows, griefs and tears,
Were but manhood-energies
Conquering what opposed their rise;
Show, from worn and clogging earth,
Soul-life germs thus gain their birth;
Clear their mental atmosphere,
Till they know our God is here.

Morning Light, tho' long we strove
In the mists that vailed thy love,
Which concealed the smiling grace
Of our God and Nature's face,

Now we see, with joy profound,
God and love our lives surround;—
Seeming frowns, their smiles of cheer,
Know our God is with us here.

---

99 LIGHT AND FREEDOM GAINING. 7.

See! the glorious morn appears—
Earth's great morn of manhood years;
Superstition's night is o'er;
Soon her dreams can vex no more.

Tho' the mists still linger round,
Ever thinning they are found;
Breaking, oft, some votary
Of the darkness is set free.

Many half-desponding souls,
While yet fear their thought controls,
Catch some feeble, glimmering gleams
Of the sunlight's coming beams.

In the vallies tho' we find
Many still are nearly blind,
All ascending, shout, with cheers,
"See! the Morning-Star appears!"

Despots quake with strange alarm,
And, to save their craft from harm,
Plunge into the densest mist,
That the light they may resist.

But the deepening tinge of gray,
Even there, reveals the day;
All their prudence-craft is vain—
Light and freedom on them gain.

---

100 SAFE IN NATURE'S FORTRESS. 7, 6.

In Nature's laws abiding,
  My soul, in triumph, sings;

And, in them well confiding,
  Defies old error's kings:
Tho' dogma-foes surround me,
  With fiercest battle-cry,
Their power can ne'er confound me;
  My walls their strength defy.

My fortress-tower can never
  Before their efforts fail;
But they, by vain endeavor,
  Exausted, I prevail:
Tho' superstition rages,
  My walls are built secure,
Of truth—the rock of ages—
  And ever shall endure.

In vain, with trumpet sounding,
  Old error's powers combine,
Each fruitless charge, rebounding,
  Breaks its own battle-line.
Thus, here in joy abiding,
  My soul, in triumph sings.
The Life Divine is guiding,
  And victory it brings!

---

101 MORNING.

7, 6. *Tune—Misssionary Hymn.*

What light is this that rises?
  What music round us rings?
'Tis morning! glad surprises
  Each waking warbler sings.
Behold! the East is glowing
  With ever-deepening gray!
'Tis on each cloud bestowing
  The tints of coming day!

Our souls, tho' long benighted,
  And racked with dreamy fear,
See now before us lighted
  The region once so drear;

And ever, round us, thinning,
  Distorting mists remove,
And "goblins" are beginning
  To shape to forms of love.

Now earth casts the reflection
  Of soul-illuming beams,
Revealing its connection
  With heaven's outflowing streams:
We see that joys supernal
  Unfold with us below;
And learn that Love Eternal
  Is conquering every woe.

A perfect fount of blessings,
  Each source of pain we see,
Which never yields distressings
  When from befoulments free;—
That ever when, in blindness,
  The streamlets we may rile,
In Nature's law of kindness,
  They bring us balm the while.

In joyous expectation,
  We wait the deepening dawn,
And fullest revelation
  When all the mists are gone;
Exulting in the measure
  Of light upon our way,
Faith finds mid sorrows, pleasure;
  It antedates the day.

---

102 NIGHT PASSING AWAY. 7, 6.

The night of superstion
  Is passing from the earth;
Man feels his new condition
  Of spiritual birth;—
His nature's life-relation
  His powers of thought commands;

The laws of new creation
  He finds within his hands.

The dreamy hosts, awaking,
  Feel the transforming power;
The despot forces, quaking,
  Are weakening every hour;
Old persecution falters,
  And, 'neath Hypocrisy,
Affects to build the altars
  Of "moral purity."

In last, despairing charges
  The foes of right engage;
But freedom's host enlarges,
  And checks their craft and rage;
And, tho' not well perceiving
  Their battle-field before,
Their blows are well retrieving
  The losses met of yore.

As morning inspiration
  The more secures its sway,
Our souls, in transformation,
  Give manly faith its play;—
In self-respect arising,
  The loves assert their right
To work to God's devising
  In manhood's Morning Light.

They open Nature's pages,
  Till Law, Divine, is found;
The fetters of the ages
  We trample on the ground;
We'll scale the towering mountains,
  Tho' stumbling by the way,
Till basking in the fountains
  Of open, beaming day.

103 THE DAY-STAR IS APPEARING. 7, 6.

The Day-Star is appearing;
  It heralds morning's dawn;
The fogs commence the clearing;
  They'll from us soon be gone;
As broken clouds, then, shining
  With rising sunbeams' glow,
They, from each golden lining,
  Shall luster on us throw.

What tho' in troubled dreaming,
  Long seemed our gloomy night,
Our life-blood often seeming
  To stagnate with affright!
The morning-beams, transforming,
  Distortions shall remove,
And manhood-life, well warming,
  Unfold in vital love.

Faith, freed, enlightened, grounded
  In natural law, divine,
No more shall be confounded,
  Nor feel its powers decline;
But, deepening, broadening, towering
  In manly majesty,
Shall welcome without cowering
  The doubt that sets it free;

His office recognizing,
  It gives the countersign;—
In confidence, well prizing
  The sentinel divine;
It finds his hand extended
  To lead it on the way,
Till darkening clouds, ascended,
  Leave unobscured the day.

We joy in the appearing
  Of manhood's Morning-Star,
And ever toward us nearing
  The day that seemed afar;

The morning inspiration
  Expands our souls with cheer:
It gives us full salvation
  From superstition-fear.

---

104 THE MOUNTAIN-TOPS ARE GLOWING. 7, 6.

The mountain-tops are glowing
  With Morning's rising beams,
And on the vallies throwing
  Their ever-brightening gleams;
And many, who were quaking
  In morbid-dream affright,
Are from their slumber waking,
  To see the dawning light.

The mountain-sides are swarming
  With those who seek the day;
Who, as they feel the warming,
  With vigor force their way:
The many just beginning
  With stumbling steps to climb;
The few where vapors thinning,
  Reveal the hights sublime.

These call, with earnest voices,
  To sleepers in the vales,
"Awake! The earth rejoices!
  The Morning Light prevails!—
Its forces serve your nature—
  Each proves a genial friend,
Who works with the 'Creator,'
  Life's every 'ill' to mend."

And tho', with dreamy terror,
  Full many still remain—
With superstition-error
  Congealing heart and brain;
Tho', for our gospel labors,
  They curses on us cast,

We know that these, our neighbors,
  Will wake to light at last.

---

105 MORNING ILLUMES THE MIND. 7, 6.

O Nature! as the cheering,
  Bright day-beams on us rise,
In grandeur new appearing,
  Thy glories meet our eyes!
We see in thee, abounding,
  Our life and joy supply;
The streams each soul surrounding,
  The fountain never dry!

We see each soul evolving
  A form for new career;
Which, lower forms dissolving,
  Rebuilds for higher sphere.
No longer are we trembling
  At fancied "demon foes,"
Whose cunning and dissembling
  O'erwhelm with final "woes."

We see, our life-endeavor,
  Tho' stumbling by the way,
The Life Divine, forever,
  Leads on in Nature's way;
No more crude aspiration,
  In thought from "sin" to free,
Would check the new "creation,"
  O Nature! wrought by thee.

No more, in pious feeling
  By fearful fancies driven,
In self-abasement kneeling,
  We pray 'gainst kindly heaven:
Our lives, now free, unguarded
  By false ideals, find
Their every act rewarded
  With light to aid the mind.

Our watchfulness employing
  To find our nature's laws,
Makes us secure, enjoying
  Repose on life's own cause:
No "evils" can befall us,
  And foes in vain assail;—
Love's law, almighty, 'round us,
  Is perfect; will prevail.

---

106 THE JOYOUS STORY. 7, 6.

How joyous is the story
  The Morning gospel sings—
That heaven's unfolding glory
  Our earth to manhood brings—
That every child of sorrow
  Our youthful earth shall rear,
Shall see a joyous morrow,
  Despite his stumbling here:

That man, each human spirit,
  And man the race, shall see
The soul-life we inherit
  From all its "evils" free—
Instructed by his "sinning"
  And sufferings, to prepare
A heavenly life; beginning
  In nature's labor-prayer.

Our souls, exulting, hear it,
  And sorrows melt away;
Our bounding hearts revere it,
  And move in freer play;
Our pains and slight privations
  In confidence we bear;—
Faith sees a full salvation
  Unfolding everywhere.

107 WE MUST TELL THE STORY. 7, 6.

Whoe'er hath seen the glory
  Of Morning's dawning light,
Must strive to tell the story
  To sleepers of the night;
His soul, with joy o'erflowing,
  Would have his neighbors share
The blessings light is throwing
  Around him everywhere.

Who feels the inspiration
  Of morning's atmosphere,
Would to earth's every nation
  Impart his lively cheer:
His soul's new life, expanding,
  Would all his fellows bless
With the new power, commanding
  A joy from old distress.

Whoe'er is plainly hearing
  The Morning-music sounds—
The lively notes of cheering,
  Which through the earth resounds,
Must seek the tones of gladness
  To pour on fellows' ears,
And wake them from the sadness
  Of superstiton-fears.

Yes! we, who know the glory,
  And lively Morning-joy,
To spread abroad the story
  Must all our powers employ;
Nor cease till all are voicing
  The soul-expanding cheer
With which the earth, rejoicing,
  Begins to charm the ear.

---

108 JOIN THE MORNING SONG 7, 6.

Let all our waking voices
  Now pass the notes along,

With which the earth rejoices
  In joyous morning song;
In lively exultation,
  We see the mists remove,
And "hells," in transformation,
  Unfolding heavenly love.

The angels, hovering o'er us,
  Now join the grand refrain—
The friends who've gone before us
  Return to earth again:
They drown all notes of sadness
  In tones of thrilling cheer;
And man awakes in gladnes,
  To see the dawn appear.

The "demons" of our dreaming
  As brothers 'round us stand;
With love fraternal beaming,
  They give the helping hand.
Our God we see with features
  Of ever-smiling grace,
Which beam on all his creatures,
  Through all the realms of space.

---

109 MORN IS DAWNING. 6, 5.

Morn is dawning! see it
  Lights the eastern sky;
Broadening, deepening, cheering
  Every open eye;
Darkness flies before it;
  Earth begins to ring
With the notes of gladness,
  Waking warblers sing.

Morn is dawning! lo it
  Clothes in radiant light
The ascending vapors
  Of the cheerless night:

Morning clouds, receiving
  Golden linings, throw
Heaven's unfolding glory
  On the world below.

Morn is dawning! purer,
  Fresher zephyrs play
With the sweetening vigor
  Of the coming day:
Larger inspirations
  Vivify the soul,
And its senses, waking,
  See our nature's goal.

Morn is dawning! gladly
  Now we join the song;
Love and joy shall triumph
  Over hate and wrong;
Rays of light are falling
  On the darkened eyes;
They shall soon illumine
  All the earth and skies.

---

110 UPWARD! SCALE THE MOUNTAINS.

6, 5. *Tune—Starlight.*

Upward! ye aspiring
  Lovers of the light!—
Reep the rising Day-Star
  Ever in your sight!
Scale the towering mountains,
  Till, in full display,
'Round you, undistorted,
  Rising sunbeams play.

Upward, press with vigor!
  Let no fears appall,
Tho', awhile, your foot-slips
  Make you sorely fall;—
Ye who, drawn by glimpses,
  Seek the glory there,

Never, in your efforts,
  Of success despair.

Upward, tho' your pathway
  Great obstructions show;
Press ye on, unheeding
  Cautions from below:
Tho' your friends beneath you,
  This, as folly, chide,
Let no timid councils
  Turn your feet aside.

Upward! just before you,
  Breaking vapors clear,
And the notes of gladness
  Chorus lively cheer!—
Listen! birds of morning
  Joyous music blend
With the joyous voices,
  Bidding you "ascend."

Upward! upward! listen
  To the triumph-tone,
While they bid you "hasten,
  Make the light your own:"
Friends have reached the region
  Of the opening day,
And are now rejoicing
  In the grand display.

---

111 THIS A WORLD OF GLADNESS. 6, 5.

Now a world of gladness
  Opens to us here,
And all clouds of sadness,
  Thinning, disappear;—
In our opening Morning
  "Evils" blessings prove—
Earth we see adorning
  In the heavenly love.

No more "wrath and chiding"
  From our God we see,
But a wisdom, guiding,
  Ever, perfectly:
Pain, we see, the teacher
  Of the laws of joy—
Freeing every creature
  From its life's alloy.

Energies, long striving
  In a half-despair,
Now, with vigor thriving,
  Join in labor-prayer;
Faith, thus firmly standing
  On great Nature's laws,
Towering and expanding,
  Grasps the living cause.

Here we see, evolving,
  Manhood master prove,
Follies, all dissolving,
  From its life remove;—
Yes! a world of gladness
  Opens to us here,
And all clouds of sadness,
  Thinning, disappear.

---

112 ANGELS WITH US HERE. 6, 5.

As the Morning deepens,
  And the light grows clear,
Angels freely join us
  In our labors here;
Each aspiring spirit
  With new life inspire,
And his waking vigor
  Warm with heavenly fire:

Circling 'round our hearth-sides
  In affliction's hour;

Nerving great achievements
  By infusing power;
Calming surging passions,
  Which would whelm the brain;—
Everywhere their presence
  Warms each vital vein.

Everywhere their loving
  Inspirations guide;—
Aid each troubled spirit,
  "Ills" to override:
When they can but whisper
  To the inner ear,
The half-wakened senses
  Catch the heavenly cheer.

But a freer converse
  With them oft we gain,
As the light, increasing,
  Flows o'er hill and plain.
Shout, ye long benighted!
  For, in day-beams' play,
Earth and heaven, before us,
  Join their hands to-day.

---

113 JOY SUPERNAL ON EARTH. 6, 5.

This is joy supernal—
  Standing in the light
Viewing love prevailing,
  Curing every blight—
Seeing racking tempests
  But expand the soul,
Adding greater vigor
  "Evils" to control.

All the sad foreboding
  Of the night are o'er—
In the joyous day-beams
  They return no more.

Grand exultings move us,
As we see appear
An evolving heaven
In each hell of fear.

"Sins," we find the teachers
Who, with kindly hand,
Point us out the pathway
To the heavenly land.
Earth we see constructing
For each child of pain
Flowing robes celestial,
Free from every stain.

Oh, the lively rapture
With which morning light,
Filling all our being,
Thrills the wondering sight!
This is joy supernal!
Who would from it stay?
Brothers, mount the highlands!
Share the light of day!

---

114 THE LIGHT COMES FLOWING ON.

Tune.—John Brown.

The morning light is dawning; see! 'tis spreading o'er the sky:
The mists of superstition all begin to break and fly,
And men begin to waken, and to see the day is nigh,
As light comes flowing on.

CHORUS.—Glory, glory, hallelujah!
Glory, glory, hallelujah!
Glory, glory, hallelujah!
The light comes flowing on.

The morbid dreams are passing from the half-awaking band

Who strive to doze in darkness while the light
flows o'er the land—
They catch some inspirations, for their friends
around them stand,
And light comes flowing on.

CHO.—Glory, glory, etc.

Our wondering eyes, now opened, see the "demons" of our dreams
Transform to beauteous angels, in the joyous
morning beams—
The friends we deemed as "lost ones," with us,
joying in the streams
Of light now flowing on.

CHO.—Glory, glory, etc.

They join our social circles, and enliven every joy;
They lighten every sorrow that would happiness
alloy;
They nerve our manly vigor all its powers to
employ,
As light comes flowing on.

CHO.—Glory, glory, etc.

We see in all around us God and Nature's smiling
face;
That there, and here within us, works their all-perfecting grace,
Which, manhood well completing, every blemish
will efface,
As light comes flowing on.

CHO.—Glory, glory, etc.

Our souls arise triumphant over every morbid fear,
For "hells" we see transforming as the light is
growing clear;—
Their fancied "demons" joining us in building
heaven here,
As light comes flowing on.

CHO.—Glory, glory, etc.

SONGS OF THE MORNING.

VOL. I.—PART II.

ORIGINAL RESPONSES TO OLD HYMNS,

INCLUDING

RESPONDING VERSIONS.

---

115 THE VIEW IN MORNING LIGHT.

C. M.

In Morning's opening light I stand,
And, with discerning eye,
Survey the fair, the blooming land,
And the effulgent sky.

Oh, the inspiring glorious scene
That rises to the sight
When fogs no more are found between
The eyes and morning light!

Sweet fields, surviving error's flood,
Stand robed in nature's green—
Where superstition-marshes stood
The fruits of truth are seen.

O'er all the well-enlightened ground,
In unobstructed play,
The rays of truth, reflected 'round,
Enliven every day.

Here dogma-creeds with poisonous breath
Can cast their blight no more;
The "victory," the "sting of death,"
Its triumphs all are o'er.

I see our Mother's loving grace
  In Nature's law-behest;
I see in all her smiling face,
  And on her bosom rest.

Old Hymn in Responding Version.

---

116 O FOR A THOUSAND TONGUES.

C. M.

O for a thousand tongues, to sing
  In loving Nature's praise—
The glories of the blossoming
  And fruitage of her grace!

Oh, loving Mother, Father, God,
  Assist me to proclaim,
And spread through all the earth abroad
  The honors of thy name.

Thy name, well known, will charm our fears,
  And bid our sorrows cease;
And, in the drooping sad one's ears,
  Will whisper hope and peace.

It breaks the fancies crude, of "sin,"
  And sets creed-victims free—
It shows their natures clean within,
  To all with eyes to see.

In Morning light thy loving voice
  Life-inspiration gives,
Which makes desponding souls rejoice,
  As each new life receives.

Hear it, ye superstitious souls!
  Your tongues 'twill then employ;
And, as awaking life controls,
  Your lame will leap for joy.

Old Hymn in Responding Version.

117 AM I A SOLDIER OF TRUTH? C. M.

Am I a soldier of the cause
  Of truth and its campaign,
And shall I swerve to win applause
  And error's favor gain?

Shall I life's higher summits scale
  On flowery beds of ease—
Against old error's force prevail
  By honeyed flatteries?

Are there no foes for me to face—
  No superstition-flood—
Will Pharisees assist the grace
  Of truth and nature's God?

Sure, if I would the cause maintain
  Of truth and Morning light,
I must, through earnest toil and pain,
  Still struggle for the right.

Truth's soldiers, in her glorious war,
  Shall conquer, tho' they die:
They see their triumph from afar,
  With Faith's discerning eye.

When truth's effulgent sun shall rise
  Its armies will combine,
And, in its beaming light-supplies,
  As victors ever shine.

Old H in Res. Ver.

---

118 WHEN I CAN READ MY TITLE CLEAR.

C. M.

When I can read my title clear
  To Nature's life-supplies,
I'll bid farewell to every fear,
  With joyous, tearless eyes.

Should creeds against my soul engage,
  And poisoned darts be hurled,
I'll smile at superstition's rage,
  And face a darkened world:

I'll shed the dawning light around
  Upon the eyes of all,
Till Morning's gospel truths, profound,
  Shall raise them from their thrall.

Then with the free, enlightened throngs,
  Whose souls their anthems raise,
We'll join the new inspiring songs
  Of God and Nature's praise.

Responding Version.

---

119 SALVATION. C. M

Salvation! O the joyful sound
  What pleasure to our ears!—
Salvation from the gloom, profound,
  Of superstition-fears:

Buried in fancies crude, of "sin"
  And "wrath divine," we lay;
But raised by Nature's grace, begin
  To see a heavenly day.

Salvation! let the echo fly
  The spacious earth around,
While all the armies of the sky
  Conspire to raise the sound.

Responding Version.

---

120 THE DAWN OF JUBILEE. C. M.

Come, sing aloud, with joyful sound,
  Of Morning gospel, free—

Proclaim to all the world around
  The dawn of jubilee!

Long lost in superstition's night,
  'Mid fears we could not flee,
Salvation comes—the Morning light—
  The dawn of jubilee!

Ye drooping souls, now raise your voice!
  Behold! your saviour see!
Ye waking prisoners, now rejoice
  In dawn of jubilee!

With rapture swell the great refrain,
  Of Morning-gospel free,
Till all the world shall ring again,
  "The dawn of jubilee!"

Let every well-enlightened soul,
  Who now the truth can see,
Exultingly the anthem roll,
  Of "dawning jubilee!"

Old H. in Res. Ver.

---

121 MORNING'S GOSPEL-TRUMPET.

C. M. *Tune—Coronation.*

Let every human ear attend,
  And every heart rejoice;
The Morning's gospel-trumpet sounds
  With an inviting voice.

Ho! all ye hungry, starving souls,
  Who feed upon the wind—
Who with tradition's childhood-toys
  Would fill a growing mind,

Eternal Wisdom here prepares
  A soul-supplying feast,
And bids your longing appetites
  The rich provision taste.

Ho! ye that pant for living streams,
  And pine away and die,
Here you may quench your raging thirst
  With springs that never dry.

The gates of Nature's gospel-grace
  Stand open night and day;—
Here all may find complete supplies,
  And drive their wants away

Old H in Res. Ver.

---

122 COME TO NATURE'S GOSPEL FEAST.

C. M.

Ye starving, superstitious souls,
  Behold a royal feast,
Where Nature spreads her bounteous store
  For each accepting guest!

She stands with open, loving arms,
  And bids you freely come,
Nor fear the priestly-wrought alarms;
  Behold! how wide the room!

Come, then, and with us freely taste
  The joys of light and love;
And, nourished by the sweet repast,
  In manly vigor move.

Then each expanding soul shall voice,
  With loud exulting tone,
The songs of those who now rejoice
  With joy so long unknown.

Thy waking spirit's opening eyes
  Shall then, in Nature, see
Thy God affording full supplies
  To all mankind, to thee.

Old H. in Res. Ver.

123 DELIGHT IN NATURE'S NAME. C. M.

How sweet thy name, O Nature! sounds
  To one who sees thee clear;
He knows thy loving life abounds
  With all that serves his cheer.

He knows it makes the wounded whole;—
  That trouble makes the breast
Expand to serve the enlarging soul,
  Who finds in labor, rest.

He knows he here can safely build,
  And needs no "hiding-place;"
That thy all-sweetening fount is filled
  With ever-flowing grace.

He knows thine every law a friend;
  O'er all its "woes" a king;
Who by its workings, in the end,
  Will blessings ever bring:

That tho' bleak fear may fill the heart
  In superstition taught,
Afflictions show thee as thou art,
  Till health in thee is sought.

Then let my powers thy love proclaim
  With every passing breath,
Till all, rejoicing in thy name,
  Find victory in "death."

Response.

---

124 GOOD IN ALL EVIL. C. M.

How grandly Nature's blessings flow!—
  The seeming false is fair;
Each poison serves our pleasure, too;
  Our sweetening, every care.

The darkest things in earth and sky
  Diffuse some rays of light;

We should inspect for joy-supply
  In every wild affright.

Our enemies, as well as friends,
  Whose love so warms our blood,
Reflect some light upon our minds,
  Revealing nature's God.

The sourness of inverted loves,
  E'en while it stings the sense,
Back to the aching vacuum moves
  Affections driven hence.

O Nature! give us light to see
  Our spirits' needed food,
And ever from the chaff to free
  The grains of real good!

Response.

---

125 ALL HAIL, THE TRUTH.

C. M. *Tune—Coronation.*

All hail, the Truth! behold he comes!
  See! errors prostrate fall!
He comes with royal diadem,
  And crowned the Lord of all!

He comes as reason's morning-beams
  Dawn on our earthly ball;
He comes! we wake from morbid dreams!
  He comes, the Lord of all!

He comes, and superstition-fears
  No more our souls appall!
He comes, the "peril" disappears!
  He comes, the Lord of all!

He comes to all—no chosen race—
  No partial remnant small;
He brings to all his sovereign grace;
  He comes, the Lord of all!

He comes with crown of manliness
For those who heed his call;
He comes! in him our souls possess
The crown and Lord of all.

"Let every kindred, every tribe
On this terrestrial ball,
To him all majesty ascribe,
And crown him Lord of all."

Then, with the mighty joyous throng
Arising from their thrall,
We'll join the grand exulting song
To Truth—the Lord of all!

Response to Old Hymn.

---

126 EARTH YIELDS A HEAVENLY HOME.

C. M.

Here joy is found! No more I'll sigh—
The Morning light has come!
It shows our world, like "that on high,"
Affords a heavenly home.

Celestial gleams on earth we know;
We find a sheltering dome
Are Nature's laws: they conquer woe,
And yield a heavenly home.

The lively inspirations 'round
Disperses lingering gloom;—
Earth glows!—her now transforming ground
Affords a heavenly home.

Response to Old H.

---

127 ASPIRATION. C. M.

While thee I seek, great Nature's power,
Be creed-taught fancies stilled;

And let this aspiration-hour
With reason's light be filled.

Thy grace to free my thoughts bestow,
Assist me while I soar;—
Let light undimmed around me flow
While I thy laws explore.

When skies from darkening mists are clear,
Thy ruling hand I see—
In dreaded "evils" blessings dear,
Conferred on all by thee.

I look, and all thy works and ways,
E'en every pain I bear,
I find thy perfect care displays,
And serves my nature's prayer.

Help me to gain the joyous hour
When light my life shall fill—
When blinding mists no more shall lower,
And hide thy loving will:

When faith's strong eye, without a tear,
Through every storm shall see;
And for the struggling feel no fear,
But know thy power will free.

Response to Old H.

---

128 ASPIRATION FOR MANHOOD-FAITH.

C. M.

Let manhood's well unfolded faith
Enlighten well my powers;—
I then shall triumph over death
In life's most clouded hours.

Through breaking mists, the gleams of light
Its youthful efforts prove,
Until its opening spirit-sight
The chill of doubts remove.

Then, joying in the strength I have,
  In confidence I'll sing,
"No victory is with the grave!
  Death has no 'vengeful sting!'"

Our nature's God gives victory
  To life of every grade;—
'Tis but the vestments drop and die,
  Life is anew arrayed.

Response to Old H.

---

129 PRAYER FOR A TRUE HEART. C. M.

O for a heart to praise my God
  With working-sympathy
Toward fellows struggling 'neath the load
  Of any slavery:

A heart that fires when grasping greed
  The despots would enthrone;
That yearns with fellows' every need,
  And makes their cause its own:

A heart whose every pulsing-beat
  Propels resistless streams
Of vital courage, to defeat
  Oppression's selfish schemes.

Old H. in Res. Ver.

---

130 AN ANGEL REACHES FROM THE GRAVE. C. M.

Now Morning light affords the faith
  To cheer the dying hours—
It shows, an angel-friend is death,
  Who aids the living powers.

We see it serve the forms it gave
  And, in full triumph, sing,

"An angel reaches from the grave,
 And not a 'monster's sting!'"

Response.

---

131 MORNING VIEW REVEALS SPIRIT-LIFE. C. M.

The once-loved form whose soul has fled,
 To-day, our thought employs,
Yet, joyous, know, the seeming "dead"
 Has risen to higher joys.

Faith melts in sight in Morning time,
 For, on the angel-shore,
We see, now born to angel-prime,
 The friend who goes before.

Then childhood-nature, cease from tears!
 The light spreads o'er the sky,
Till to our reason's view appears
 The realms of life on high.

Response.

---

132 A VOICE OF LOVE FROM THE TOMBS. C. M.

Hark! from the tombs a joyful sound,
 While light falls on the eye:
"Ye trembling souls, within the ground
 'Tis but the vestments lie!

"Life's higher spheres the spirits tread,
 And wield untrammeled powers;
From whence, returning oft, they shed
 Their light on earthly hours.

"Ye stand, amid the seeming gloom,
 In endless life, secure;—
Your nature's God permits no 'doom'
 The spirit to 'immure:'

"The all-encircling perfect grace,
  Through Nature's law-supplies,
Will perfect all to see his face
  On earth or in the skies."

Response.

---

133 DEATH, LIFE'S DEFENSE. C. M.

O man, to delve in creeds forbear!
  Now cast thine eyes on high!
The opening day is not afar—
  It lights the Eastern sky.

Reflect! thy soul doth greatly crave
  Above the mists to mount,
And see that the long-dreaded grave
  Ne'er closes life's account:

That death but serves for life's defense—
  To lovingly compel
Each outworn part to move from hence,
  Nor prove the being's hell.

Thy flesh-obstructions thus, with care,
  The vital fires consume;—
"Destruction" is but life-repair;
  It works beyond the tomb.

Response.

---

134 DEATH, LIFE'S PIONEER. C. M.

Why do we mourn departed friends,
  Or see in death, alarms?
'Tis only superstition, sends
  A dread of Nature's arms.

All life is tending upward, too,
  As fast as time can move;

Nor should we wish the hours more slow
  Which perfects all in love.

We should but joy when life's full day
  Man ripens for the tomb,
And know 'tis but the vestments lay
  Within the seeming gloom.

Each joy with which our lives are blest,
  Each grand life-quickening breath,
Each aspiration of the breast
  Is pioneered by death:

Each life unfolds by lower forms
  Dissolving for its sake;
Life's angel sways "destruction-storms,"
  Their forces builders make.

Then, in the light, let goblin-fears
  No more our bosoms sway,
But, joyous, will new forms and years
  Our honored, outworn clay.

Response.

---

135 THE MORNING'S RESCUE. C. M.

Plunged in a darkness nigh despair,
  In misty creeds we lay,
Where to our nature's childhood's night
  Scarce reached a glimmering ray.

Blind impulse-struggles broke our peace,
  And, in a mighty grief,
We strove with drooping energies
  To find a true relief.

Fraternal love inflamed by fear
  The wild resentments led,—
In strife to save our fellows' soul,
  Their bodies burned and bled.

But morning light fell on the plains,
  The fogs began to break,
And from our frenzied, morbid dreams,
  Our souls began to wake.

Then, with the mist-distortions o'er,
  Our God could show his face;
And what to fears a frown appeared,
  We saw was smiling grace.

Now rocks and hills, and angel bands
  Assist our nature's lays,
While, in exulting joyous songs,
  We God and Nature praise.

Response to Old H

---

136 COME, HOLY SPIRIT. C. M.

Come, Holy Spirit, heavenly Dove,
  With all thy quickening powers,
Kindle a flame of trustful love
  In hearts which fear devours.

In vain they sing old dogma-songs,
  In vain they strive to rise,
They languish, shrivel, on their tongues,
  And such devotion dies.

Oh! shall our brethren ever live
  At this poor dying rate—
With fears congealing love to thee,
  While thine is still so great?

Come, Holy Spirit, heavenly Dove,
  With all thy quickening powers,
And wake their nature's deeper love,
  That it may join with ours.

Old H. in Res. Ver.

137 NATURE'S GOD APPEALS TO THE CREED-BOUND. C. M.

Ye creed-bound, nature's God regard;
He clearly speaks to-day—
He calls, in open science-word,
From dogmas' darkened way.

'Mid blinding mists you ne'er can rest,
Nor feel a real peace;
The aspirations of your breast
In darkness find no ease.

To foster discord—build a "hell,"
Why will you persevere,
When in the light you all may dwell
Of joys serene and clear?

Why will you in the darkened ways
Of superstition go—
In painful struggles spend your days
With mere imagined "woe?"

Turn to the light, and you shall live
In Nature's flowing grace!
The dawning day begins to give
The light to see her face.

Look to her all-perfecting word;
'Twill banish dreams of "sin,"
And show, in you your nature's "Lord"
Well works his will divine.

Old H in Res. Ver.

---

138 COME, DOGMA'S VICTIM, LOOK TO NATURE. C. M

Come, dogma's victim, in whose breast
A thousand fears revolve,

Come, with your sense of "guilt" oppressed,
  And make this firm resolve:

"I'll look to Nature, and, within
  The light her laws disclose,
Review my creeds—my thoughts of 'sin,'
  And causes of my 'woes:'

"Erect in manliness, I'll claim
  My right to Nature's grace—
To know her laws and make the same
  My blemishes efface:

"I'll to her sovereign power approach,
  And ask that it bestow
On man the same perfecting touch
  That serves all life below.

"Perhaps her great unfolding-laws
  Will serve my nature's prayer;
I'll fully trust that folly-flaws
  Her workings will repair.

"I shrivel 'neath my chilling creeds,
  I am resolved to try
If Nature cannot to my needs
  Afford complete supply."

Response to Old H.

---

139 I HEARD THE VOICE OF JESUS. C. M.

I heard the voice of Jesus say,
 "Ye love me? freely feed
My tender lambs—the famishing—
  Destroy the reign of greed."

I looked to Jesus, and I saw
  A loving brother there,
Who for the weak and sorrowing
  Wrought, ever, labor-prayer.

My soul responded earnestly
  To his fraternal call;
And nations I beheld profess
  To "crown him Lord of all."

I said, Behold the time has come!
  Heaven's kingdom now is born!
I sought their aid, to work for him,
  They laughed my thought to scorn.

Then to the circle of the "saints"—
  The church—with hope I turned,
It rated me an "infidel"
  My aspiration spurned.

With saddened soul, I turned again
  And listened for his word:
Are these thy friends? he answered, "Nay;
  Not all who say 'Lord! Lord!'"

Response.

---

140 SAVIOURS NOT ALWAYS TO BE MARTYRED. C. M.

Behold! while saviours of mankind
  Must suffer still for thee,
The dawning lights the public mind;
  From error's power 'twill free.

Each life-divine, through suffering, makes
  The despots' pillars bend,
Till, with co-workers joined, he breaks
  The powers which truth would rend.

And tho' the slaves who by his aid
  Were saved, unite their cries
In clamor 'gainst the sacred head
  Who comes more fully wise,

And, in the former martyr's name,
  Rekindle martyr-fires

For every one in whom the same
  Illumined love inspires,

Yet sons of light shall break the chain
  Which manhood-powers confine;
O freedom-toiler! not in vain
  Are lives of love, like thine.

Response to Old Hymn.

---

141 THE TRUE PREACHER'S WORK. C. M.

Let preachers from old dreams awake,
  And real gospel give—
From human nature's loving God
  The charge divine receive.

'Tis not a work of small import
  They take upon their hands—
To light the minds and warm the hearts
  Of eager, listening bands:

The passive natures, by their words
  Are shaped for weal or woe—
In love, to bless, or bigotry,
  To blight where'er they go.

Response to Old H.

---

142 REJOICING IN MORNING GOSPEL. L. M.

O how a glance of opening day
Old superstition sweeps away,
Till the inflowing life divine,
Awaking, fills this soul of mine!

With racking fears no more I'll quake,
Tho' earth with wild convulsions shake;
"Destructive" powers, I know, combine
To serve all life; to ripen mine.

The loads of sorrow man has felt
In new evolving joys will melt—
In Nature's word each glowing line
Declares her forces serving mine.

Her judgments now with joy I hear
They banish "demons," "goblins," fear;
For each award gives perfect sign
Of kindness toward this life of mine.

Her great design, outworking deeds
Will fill all aspiration-needs—
Make dross to serve, and then refine.
And well perfect this life of mine.

Old H. in Res. Ver.

---

143 DELIGHT IN MORNING GOSPEL.

L. M.

Far from my thoughts old creeds be gone,
Let my religious hours alone!
As I our Morning gospel see,
I need no visit more from thee:

My heart is warmed with purer fire;
Thy torch I can no more desire—
The light is streaming from above;
It fills my soul with joy and love.

O Nature! what delicious fare!
How sweet thine entertainments are!
When will the dreamers wake and know
The fullness of their perfect flow?

Old H. in Res. Ver.

---

144 NATURE'S LIFE A FOUNT OF SWEETNESS. L. M.

Sweet is the joy thy power doth bring,
O Nature! we thy praises sing!

We see thy life in Morning light,
And waken from the shades of night.

Thy love each day gives sweetening rest,
Tho' weighty cares may seize the breast;
It tunes the heart in joyous sound
To all the harmonies around.

We triumph in her life and Lord!—
Thy works express thy loving word!—
Thy truth and grace there fully shine,
Eternal, natural, divine.

We freely share a glorious part—
The streams o'erflow each open heart,
And in abounding floods are shed
Upon the light-encircled head.

At last, in unobstructed flow,
E'en as above 'twill serve below;
And every world give sweet employ,
And prove a world of perfect joy.

Responsive Version.

---

145 I FOUND THE TRUE, ALMIGHTY FRIEND. L. M.

O happy day, when Nature's voice
First reached my ear and helped my choice,
Where I could really rejoice
In a divine, Almighty friend!

In darkening mists' distorted light
I saw, misshapen to my sight,
My nature "fallen," God a blight,—
Not a divine, Almighty friend.

My drooping soul then cast around
Its eyes, in agony profound,

It saw all Nature's fruits abound,
But no divine, Almighty friend.

Friends bade me gain the "sovereign grace"
Through "one who suffered in my place."
My soul, revolting, sought embrace
From a divine, Almighty friend:

I could not real justice see
In guiltless sacrifice for me;—
It pierced my heart; I longed to flee
To a divine, Almighty friend.

Then Nature's voice fell on my ear:
"The real God, you seek, is here!"
The breaking fogs began to clear;—
I found the true Almighty Friend.

Response.

---

146 LINGERING SUPERSTITION-FANCIES. L. M.

While morning light light is flowing round,
O Nature! fancies dark are found—
Of "sin" and a "corrupting fall;"
And many souls they still enthrall.

To feeble, opening infant-thought
These superstition-fears are taught,
Till chilled, contracted, is the heart,
And reason dwarfed in every part.

Then hungering sense of spirit need
Is left on husks like these to feed,
With sense of "guilt" for which alone
Enslaving priestly-faiths "atone."

Thus morbid fancies break their peace;
Thy light alone can give them ease—
Can rescue faith from what devours,
And wake and free the manhood-powers.

Give us, who see the light, the zeal
To work for human nature's weal—
To help our fellows gain the hight
Of undistorted Morning light.

Response.

---

147 NATURE'S LOVING KINDNESS. L. M.

Awake, my soul, to joyful lays,
And sing our mother Nature's praise!
She justly claims a song from thee—
Her loving kindness, O how free!

She saw thee lost in darkest night,
And shed upon thee Morning light.
It rescued from thy darkened state;
Her loving kindness, O how great!

When countless hosts of dogma-foes
Thy needed freedom did oppose,
She armed with truth, and led along;
Her loving kindness, O how strong!

When Nature seemed a dismal cloud,
Where dangers, gathering, thundered loud,
She gave her laws into thy hand;
Her loving kindness, O how grand!

Tho' struggling wants did often start
Tempestuous passions in the heart,
She forced the balance when forgot;
Her loving kindness changes not.

When life appeared a gloomy vale,
Where vital powers at last must fail,
She showed that, through the waning breath,
Her loving kindness rules in "death;"—

That in a world of perfect light
The ripened spirit sees aright;

And sings, with widely-opened eyes,
Her loving kindness in the skies.

Old H. in Res. Ver.

---

148 OUR NATURE NEEDS NO HIDING-PLACE. L. M.

Hail, Morning light! Thy dawn began
To rescue dark, benighted man
From fears that sought to shun thy grace,
In dogmas' dark, soul-hiding place.

In misty creeds, my tortured eye
Beheld our God uplifting, high,
A vengeful rod to smite our race;
And then I sought a "hiding place."

While darkness much my soul did blight,
I clung to it and feared the light;
I madly strove in its embrace
To find my "needed" "hiding place."

I trembled when the dawning day
Shot gleams of light upon my way:
It seemed the "flames of hell," in chase,
While still I had no "hiding place."

With "vengeance" rushing on my view,
Within the thickest mists I flew;
But soon the light increased apace,
Till this I found no "hiding place."

Then Nature's loving voice I heard;
Truth's angel in her "flames" appeared;
He freed my eyes from mists' embrace;
I needed then no "hiding place."

Now all my fellows I would tell,
What darkened fancy deems a "hell,"
Is light to aid a darkened race;
Our nature needs no "hiding place.

Old H. in Res. Ver.

149 NOT ASHAMED OF NATURE. L. M.

O Nature! shall it ever be—
Man's "pious" pride ashamed of thee,
While all, thy glory so displays
That grandest angels sing thy praise?

Ashamed of Nature? man despise
The fount of all his life-supplies!
Oh, shall the mists forever hide
The lovely light by thee supplied!

Ashamed of Nature, as "depraved,"
When only Nature's grace hath saved
Some vision-power, to see the light
While dogma-vapors vail the sight.

Ashamed of Nature! just as soon
Let morning-dawn disown its noon!—
The dawning aspirations, all,
For noon-day light on Nature call.

Ashamed of Nature! *man* thus chide
The forms of love in which abide
The great All-Father-Mother-Soul,
Whose love and wisdom all control!

Nay! Man, awake? and, from the plain,
Ascend the mounts, where you may gain
The light, full, undistorted, free,
The Nature will *your glory* be.

Old H in Res. Ver.

---

150 JUST AS I AM. L. M.

Just as I am, I need no plea,
O nature's God! thy work in me
Is life divine that would be free;—
It ably strives to gain the room.

Just as I am, I know that not
A blunder can my nature blot—
Thy loving law shall cleanse each spot
When it succeeds in gaining room.

Just as I am, I cannot doubt,
Thy perfect law, within, without,
Will ripened manhood bring about,
And make itself abundant room.

Just as I am, thy law can find
How to enlighten well the mind,
Till darkening mists no more can blind,
Its working power will gain the room.

Just as I am, I do believe
That perfect grace I do receive,
All imperfections to relieve;
My nature strives to make it room.

Just as I am, I feel its power
At work within me every hour.
Faith grounded well to heaven doth tower;
I shall not fail to make it room.

Response to Old H.

---

151 A CALL TO GOD AND NATURE'S PRAISE. L. M. *Tune—Old Hundred.*

From all that dwell below the skies,
Let life's true joyous anthems rise—
Let God and Nature's praise be sung
Through every land by every tongue!

Abundant are their blessings poured;
Abundant care their laws afford;
And all supremely will adore
When wisdom wakes to know them more.

Their loving, providential care
Spreads teeming bounties everywhere;

And bids them serve our life's demands,
Responsive to our active hands.

Let all that live in concert sing,
And labor-worship incense bring ;
With heaven and all the worlds proclaim
The co-eternal, loving name.

O sons of earth, benighted long,
The morn is dawning ! join the song !
Let faith its working triumphs raise,
And fill our world with active praise !

Responsive Version.

---

152 RESPECT FOR EARTH AND BASIC LOVES. L. M.

My God, permit me not to be
A stranger to myself and thee—
Oh, never let my conscience rove
In disrespect of any love.

When aspiration spurns the earth
In misty view of heavenly birth,
Teach me I need the things below,
That I in them my God may know.

Teach me to know the fleshly-sense
Nurse of young spirit-forms, and hence
That to obey thy voice divine
No other joy I should resign.

Thus earth, the base of life, well known,
My soul can ne'er its joys disown ;
But, with a well-enlightened mind,
My God and heaven I here shall find.

Old H. in Res. Ver.

153 FEAR OF DEATH. L. M.

Why should we start and fear to die?
  What timorous ones we mortals are?
Death is the gate to higher joys,
  And yet we fear to enter there:

The creed-made sting and dying strife
  Start our affrighted souls away,
And we shrink back to earthly life,
  And cling to feeble, outworn clay.

If Nature's truth our souls could meet,
  They then would stretch their wings in haste,
Fly fearless through "death's iron gate,"
  And prove it GOLDEN as they passed.

Responsive Version.

---

154 NO ROAD LEADS TO DEATH. L. M.

There is no road that leads to death—
  No dark destruction anywhere,
True wisdom shows us Nature's path
  Is life for every traveler.

In open light we see that loss
  Can ne'er occur in Nature's hand;—
"Death" is but form-repair; the dross,
  Refined, rebuilds at God's command.

Ye fearful souls that shrink and faint,
  Your God hath made your triumph sure!—
The "demons" of your fear-complaint
  From all destruction will secure!

No hope's true central wish is vain—
  It wins, tho' mists may hide the view;—
Life's yearning will its goal attain;
  'Tis linked with God! 'tis ever true!

Response.

155 NATURE'S HOUR OF PRAYER.

L. M. *Tune—Sweet Hour of Prayer.*

Sweet hour of prayer, of Nature's prayer—
Of earnest work beneath her care,
Which, making all my wishes known,
Secures her work to aid my own!
When waking wants would cause me grief
I turn to thee and find relief,
And free myself from every snare
By Nature's earnest labor-prayer.

Sweet hour of prayer, of labor-prayer,
Thy wings doth each petition bear
To Nature's living, loving cause,
And answers gain from Nature's laws.
'Tis thus she bids me seek her face,
And gain her providential grace,
And rise triumphant o'er each care
By thy great power, sweet Nature's prayer.

Sweet hour of prayer, of labor-prayer,
Thy aid supports me everywhere!—
By thee I scale life's mountain hight,
And gain a view in clearer light,
And, in the rays there shed around,
In future joys gain faith profound,
And on the earth a heaven prepare
By thy kind aid, sweet labor-prayer!

Response.

---

156 THE NEW BIRTH. C. P. M.

Tune—Willoughby, or Hedding.

I woke to morning's gospel-sound
While superstition-meshes bound
  My aspirations' flow;
I scaled the mounts, high o'er the plain,
Then feeling dragged me down again
  Into the mists below.

I heard the dogma-thunders roll,
And on my chilled and struggling soul,
  A dark oppressive load
Of mixed emotions void of cheer—
Consistency disowned and fear,
  Seemed as the "wrath of God."

Then breaking mists revealed full well
The mountain-tops, where sunshine fell,
  And, rallying my powers,
With stumblings, finally did gain
The hights where light was clear and plain,
  And joyed in freedom's hours.

My nature's life, new-born that day,
Rejoices in the genial play
  Of loves in harmony;
And, in the light's unfailing fount,
Would urge my fellows all to mount,
  And its full glory see.

Response.

---

157 THE PAST, PRESENT, AND FUTURE.

C. P. M. *Tune—Willoughby, or Ganges.*

Tho' on a little point of land
In Nature's boundless field, I stand,
  Yet I am sensible
That universal loving grace,
Which rules the mighty realms of space,
  Doth serve our earth as well.

O Nature's life, my God thou art!
Thou dost within this atom-heart
  Eternal laws express!
Dost give the power to wield their weight,
And use their forces to create
  True balance—righteousness:

Did'st teach my inmost soul to pray
To Nature's life in Nature's way,
  And when the answers came,
Tho' still in superstition's mist,
With powers unconscious to assist,
  Despite its sense of "blame."

Be it my leading business here
To make thy light, O Nature! clear
  To souls in fog immured—
To show that the "creative" will
A loving purpose doth fulfill—
  That "ills" will all be cured;

That then thy light, which all receive,
Completed heaven to earth shall give,
  Nor aspirations rove
To distant worlds to find delight,
But earth, well ripened, in our sight,
  Shall bloom with perfect love.

Response to Old H.

---

158 TIME'S FLIGHT, AND ITS LESSONS.

C. P. M. *Tune—Willoughby, or Meribah.*

My days, my weeks, my months, my years
Are but the breaths of spirit-spheres,
  And whisper as they roll,
"Time for thy spirit only keeps
The form till ripened, when it reaps
  And garners well the soul."

In open light—no fogs between,
The grave is but the cradle seen
  Of Nature's nursery:
Benighted man, thy life is bliss!—
The song thy mother sings is this:
  "No thing of life can die."

Sleep while the shades around you fall,
But let no morbid dreams appall '
  And, with the ending night.
When with her voice of love, so true,
She calls, awake to life anew,
  Rejoicing in the light.

Response to Old H.

---

159 LIFE'S GREAT IMPORT. C. P. M.

Tune—Wiloughby, or Hedding.

And am I born to never die!—
Is "death" but shedding husks, to fly,
  At Nature's kind decree,
And bask in life's completer plains—
In joys celestial, free from pains—
  In true felicity!

How joyful, then, ought I to live!
No earthly "woe" should make me grieve!
  Should use my house of clay
With manly zeal and faithful care,
To make its life the soul prepare—
  Well ripen —for that day.

No room for superstition-fear,
While in the light, unfolding here,
  Our "ills" so soon are gone:
While nature's God leads on before,
Makes "woes but serve to ope the door
  For life to take its throne.

Let manly faith my thoughts employ—
Show the unfolding laws of joy,
  Which ne'er shall have an end:
Thus here begin my heavenly place,
And introduce the brighter days
  I shall with angels spend.

Response to Old Hymn.

160 WE GIVE THE WINDS OUR FEARS.

S. M.

We give the winds our fears,
And stand no more dismayed;
God's law within our life appears,
Well ruling heart and head.

The stormy waves may roll,
And sweep across our way,
It gives the power which may control
Till these shall serve our day.

No heaviness of heart
Can weigh our spirits down:
Life's law reacts till cares impart
New joys our lives to crown.

What tho' the misty creeds
Of superstition's night
Still linger 'round? our nature's needs
Are warmed by morning light!

We joyously obey
The natural-law commands;
The power which these for us may sway
Is placed within our hands.

The light to us hath brought,
In vision bright and clear,
A faith above the childish thought,
We give the winds our fear!

Response.

---

161 THE ALL IN ALL. S. M.

O God of nature—Love,
To thee, to thee we call;
Each soul doth in thy being move,
For thou art All-in-All.

Thy conscious grace can cheer
  In dungeons tho' we dwell;
'Tis paradise to know thee here;
  To doubt thy presence, hell.

The smilings of thy face
  How amiable they are!—
'Tis heaven to rest in thine embrace,
  And no where else but there.

With angels, worlds unknown,
  To thee we owe our bliss;
Thy mighty life can joy enthrone
  While tempests 'round us hiss.

Thou sea unbounded—Love!—
  Where all our pleasures roll;
Thou circle where the passions move,
  And center of the soul,

To thee our yearnings fly
  With infinite desire;
Tho' in the darkening mists we lie
  Thy light shall raise us higher.

Old Hymn in Responding Version.

---

162 FRIENDSHIP'S TIE. S. M.

Blest tie of life, that binds—
  Thou true fraternal love!
The fellowship of kindred minds
  Is like the feast above:

In Nature's loving tone
  It pours united prayers;—
Life's prompting aims, its hopes are one;
  They lighten all our cares.

True friendship soothes our "woes;"
  It comforts everywhere

While for each other's sorrow flows
  The sympathizing tear.

Tho' when true friends must part
  It gives us inward pain,
Yet often, in each yearning heart,
  In loves we meet again.

When from the borrowed "woe"
  Of dreaded "sin" we're free
Our friendship shall unbroken flow,
  And all its blessings see.

Old H. in Res. Ver.

---

163 THE FOUNT OF GRACE. S. M.

Behold! the fount of grace
  To every soul is near—
Kind Nature, with her smiling face,
  To answer real prayer.

For needs, ask when thou wilt;
  Be confident and bold;
No labor-prayer is wasted, spilt;—
  Supplies she'll not withhold.

Thus Nature, in thy faith,
  Our wills shall blend with thine;
And we shall find that e'en in death
  Thy bounteous blessings shine.

Response.

---

164 GRACE FIRST AND LAST. S. M.

Grace! 'tis a charming sound!—
  The music of the spheres;
Heaven sends the echo all around,
  And earth, responding, cheers.

Grace serves in Nature's way,
  Perfecting earth and man;
And all the steps of its display
  Reveal the perfect plan.

Grace makes the wandering feet,
  Evolving, find the road
Where manhood's conscious sense shall meet
  Its *real*, loving God.

Grace *then* shall fully crown
  Its work of youthful days—
Heaven's dome complete—its topmost stone
  Upon our earth shall raise.

ponding Version.

---

165 SEEKING THE SPIRIT OF TRUE PRAYER. S. M.

Thy praying spirit breathe,
  O Nature! power impart
From creed-entanglements, beneath,
  To free each yearning heart.

Our waking faith sustain
  Till dawning light, possessed,
Shall clearly show thy laws will gain
  For all, their needed rest:

That from their work shall come
  The power to fully seize
The joys of earth and heavenly home—
  Perfected life and peace.

Then never shall we rove
  Through blinding mists abroad;
But, freed by Nature's light and love,
  We'll dwell with nature's God.

Old H. in Res. Ver.

166 HEAVENLY JOY ON EARTH. S. M.

Who know our nature's Lord,
  Come, let your joys be known ;
Join in a song, with sweet accord,
  To see your hearts his throne.

Let those refuse to sing
  Who have not seen our God,
But ye may make earth's vallies ring
  With joys proclaimed abroad.

The earth for you now yields
  A thousand sacred sweets ;
It opens here the heavenly fields,
  With heavenly blessings greets.

Then let our songs abound,
  And every tear be dry !—
Our earth is all heaven's joyous ground,
  And joins the heavens on high !

Old H. in Res. Ver.

---

167 COME SING OUR EARTHLY HEAVEN

S. M. *Tune—No Sorrow There.*

Come, sing our earthly heaven—
  The joys that here are nigh !—
This to the soul when cares oppress
  Gives conquering energy.

CHORUS—Our sorrows light appear,
      And ever end in cheer ;
    To manly faith with open eye
      Our sorrows light appear.

Inspired, our souls will see
  That through all dreaded " woes "—

Through pains and deaths of germic forms
  Our manhood forms arose.

Cho.—Our sorrows, etc.

Faith's music in the ears,
  In songs exulting given,
Makes earth, with all her crowding cares.
  The vestibule of heaven.

Cho.—Our sorrows, etc.

Counterparting Response.

---

168 WE ARE NOT BORN TO DIE. S. M.

We are not born to die!
  Nor lay our bodies down
Until our spirits need to fly
  And make the heavens their own:
The form outworn is made
  A clog to life and thought;
We give it other forms to aid,
  By Nature ne'er forgot.

Nor far from earth we go;
  But still most dear shall be
The friends beloved; their joy and woe
  We share in sympathy.
Great Nature's trumpet sound
  Calls all of life to rise
To higher plains, where, newly crowned,
  It scans the larger skies.

In open light a doubt
  Can never pain the breast—
The welcome friend we cast not out,
  For by it all are blest:
While fear from us is driven,
  It aids our Saviour well—
The Wisdom—which constructs a heaven,
  Transforming every hell.

O ye who dread the grave—
  Who fear the soul can "die,"
Or that the "creeds" alone can save
  From "final misery,"
When wise, your souls will know
  Life's angel leads us here—
That death conducts from transcient woe
  To Nature's higher sphere.

Response to Old H.

---

169 BLOW YE THE TRUMPET, BLOW.

H. M. *Tune—Lenox.*

Blow ye the trumpet, blow,
  With loud exulting sound!—
Let all the nations know
  To earth's remotest bound
The dawn of jubilee has come;
Return! ye wanderers, return!

Ye slaves of darkness-creeds
  And superstition-fright,
Now, answering your needs,
  See! Nature sends her light!—
The dawn of jubilee has come!
Return to freedom's light, return!

Ye who from priestlings think
  To gain a heavenly day,
See! from their creeds they shrink,
  Explaining them away:
The dawn of jubilee has come!
Return to Nature's light, return!

The living gospel hear,
  Proclaiming Nature's grace!
Before you see appear
  You Mother-Saviour's face!
The dawn of jubilee has come!
Return to Nature! now, return!

H. in Res. Ver.

170 RISE, MORNING SUN.

H. M. *Tune—Lenox.*

Rise, morning sun! thy rise
  Shall banish manhood's night,
Illume and warm our skies
  Till free from chilling blight!
O chase these dismal mists away,
And bring the bright millennial day!

Long, hiding nature true,
  Old error-fogs have lain.
These, to our human view,
  Distorted all the plain,
And aspirations led astray
Till checked by passion's impulse-play.

Thy fullest rays send down
  Each darkened land to greet,
Till every despot's crown
  Is 'neath its victims' feet:
Till kings and priests, beneath thy sway,
Shall nature's law and God obey.

Then on our earth, complete,
  Heaven's kingdom shall appear;
Then each shall fellows greet
  With true fraternal cheer,
And fully Nature's grace display,
And worship God in Nature's way.

Response.

---

171 ARISE, MY SOUL, ARISE.

H. M. *Tune—Lenox.*

Arise, my soul, arise
  From superstition-fear!—
Thy true, divine supplies
  In Nature's life appear;

Upon her laws thy surety stands,
And these are placed within thy hands.

They ever work in love
  For human nature's need—
In earth and heaven above,
  All men and angels feed:
They serve abundantly our race,
And all that lives, within their place.

Then let our nature's prayers
  In Nature's channels flow,
And bear away all cares,
  And folly-dreams of "woe;"
And know that "sins"—mistakes, supply
Life-light to save, that none may die.

Thy God within thee reigns;
  Thou art his cherished child:
His loving care retains
  Control of passions wild;—
Behold, with an unclouded eye,
Thy nature's God gives full supply!

Old Hymn in Responding Version.

---

172 THE ALL-PERFECTING NAME.

H. M. *Tune—Lenox.*

O that all earth could see,
  And, with the angels joined,
From superstition free,
  The *real* Saviour find!—
Could break from creeds which hide her face,
And rest in Mother Nature's grace!

O Mother! thou art found
  The joy of highest heaven!
In thee doth love abound,
  Which to each soul is given;

Who know thy love salvation have!
To understand is to believe!

Thy all-perfecting name
  Charms all the hosts above;
They see thy gracious aim
  Successful ever prove;
Tho' transient pains must teach the road,
Through hells, unto the heaven abode.

Thy name the darkened hears,
  Half tuned to harmony,
While ringing in his ears
  Is discord's "litany."
E'en then in higher powers' employ
He finds uncomprehended joy.

Response.

---

173 NATURE'S ABUNDANT GRACE. P. M.

O Nature! thy grace, from the infinite fountain,
Flows over our race, overflows every mountain;
Each earthy obstruction, the *seeming* pollution,
It washes away in desolving dilution.
Hallelujah! the stream is abundant forever!
Heaven's rays in it beam, and it serves each endeavor.

Ler praise to its power most freely be given;
For praise to its power is the anthem of heaven:
Around the whole earth let us tell the glad story,
Till each human soul shall exult in its glory.
Hallelujah! the stream is abundant forever!
Heaven's rays in it beam, and it serves each endeavor

O life-stream flow on! thy working is glorious!
Whate'er acting on thou art ever victorious!
At last thy full flow, to each clime, land and nation,
Shall fully bestow perfect manhood-salvation:
Hallelujah! the stream is abundant forever!
Heaven's rays in it beam, and it serves each endeavor.

When in manhood we stand—all our race on that shore,
We'll strike vigorous hands in its serf evermore,
Then range the bright fields on the banks of the river,
And sing hallelujah forever and ever.
Hallelujah! the stream is abundant forever!
Heaven's rays in it beam, and it serves each endeavor.

Old H in Res. Ver.

---

174 LIFE TRIUMPHANT P. M.

Let your glad voices ascend to the sky!
For Nature is life, and her sons ne'er can die!
Dark are the fancies and fears that have bound us,
And lurid the hues they have cast on the grave;
But darkness now scatters, the light breaks around us,
And shows Nature's power fully able to save:
Lift all your voices in triumph on high!
Sing "Nature is life, and her sons shall not die.'

Nature and God join our anthems of joy;
Their life is our own, and death does not destroy:
Sad seems the hour when we, parting in sorrow,
Leave crumbling, dissolving, the form of a friend,
But Day-Beams, before us, reveal a to-morrow,
When every fond life shall, unfolding, ascend.
Lift, then, your voices in triumph on high,
For Nature prevails and no life e'er can die.

Well may we join with the angels to-day,
Since light, dawning on us, has opened the way.
Light, as it chases the gloom from before us,
Reveals them our kindred—the friends we have mourned,
On love-wings celestial now hovering o'er us;
In ripe love and wisdom completely adorned.
Join, then, the concert of triumph on high!
For theirs is our triumph! we never shall die!

Responding Version.

175 THE SOUL'S JOY IMMORTAL

L. P. M. *Tune—Greenfield.*

I'll joy in Nature while I've breath;
Assured her power, supreme in "death,"
Immortal makes my living powers:
My days of joy shall ne'er be past,
But, rising through all storms at last,
My soul with nature's God endures.

How blest the man whose open eye
Beholds his God, in earth and sky,
Dispensing kindness e'en in pain;
He works in manly faith, secure,
He rights the wrongs which make us poor,
And triumphs o'er the oppressors' train.

Her light pours eyesight on the blind—
The creed-bedarkened, drooping mind,
And gives his morbid conscience peace:
It brings full rescue from distress
To all whom darkened powers oppress,
And gives the prisoners sweet release.

I'll joyous work with earthly breath,
Nor cease when that is lost in "death,"
But then my freer, nobler powers,
With all obstructions from them cast,
Shall freely work in fields more vast
While nature's life, our God, endures.

Responding Version.

---

176 I WOULD NOT LIVE ALWAY. 11.

I would not live alway; I ask not to stay
Where mists of old errors can darken our way;
The gleams of true soul-light that dawn on us here
Invite us all onward to life's higher sphere.

I would not live alway, 'mid frettings of "sin"—
Where conscience must war with the soul-life within;
Where the vague sense of "pardon" scarce quiets our fears,
And leaves our thanksgivings embittered with tears.

I would not live alway, no welcome the tomb:
My flesh worn, and weary, shall find there no gloom;
Each atom, at Nature's new call, shall arise,
To build up new forms for the earth and the skies

Ah, who would live alway, when Nature and God
Thus beckon the soul to its blissful abode,
Where the rivers of pleasure flow o'er the bright plains,
And love in its joyous maturity reigns:

Where brethren, creed-parted, at last all shall meet,
Transported with joy all their kindred to greet,
And the anthems of rapture exultingly roll,
While hope's full fruition encircles the soul.

Responding Version.

---

177 NATURE'S ASSURANCE. 11.

I once was a stranger to morn's dawning rays;
A feeling of danger held downward my gaze;
Friends bade me look up to the heavens and see,
The heavens seemed frowning with darkness on me.

I saw, deeply grieving, "God's grace could supply
But favorites, leaving all others to die."
His law "*tortured* those it neglected to free;"
And, "cursing my fellows, was threatening me."

Vague terror was spreading a pall o'er my hours,
Whose darkness was shedding a blight on my powers;

I wished from my conscious existence to flee,
But thinning mists broke and the light fell on me.

A mountain all glowing with clear open light,
Before me was throwing its rays on my sight;
I scaled it; each leaf of each beckoning tree
Revealed nature's God kindly smiling on me.

In life's highland regions, I saw that divine
Is life; all its legions; this portion of mine:
That "death" is ascending of spirits set free;
And this at the last my own "death-song" shall be.

Response.

---

178 HOW SHALL WE ENLIGHTEN THE DARKENED. 11.

O what shall we do that may carry the grace
Of morn's dawning rays to our long-darkened race,
Till each fellow-soul it completely redeems
From all superstition which hides the day-beams.

How joyous the soul whom the light has set free!
He sees, loving Nature! his union with thee;
He walks in the glow of his God's loving face;
And finds his his own nature a fountain of grace.

Heaven's laws he can boast, for their glory and
power
Impel his life-forces; control every hour;
In soul-elevation he raises his head,
And greets the salvation from darkness and dread.

Man's wisdom is lord of whate'er gives offense;
The breath of its word casts obstructions from
hence:
It proves a true saviour, well able to do
Each soul the great favor of making anew:

Evolving, we see that it mounts to its throne;
And manhood made free and its powers being
known,

All shadows of sadness its joy soon relieves;
Imparting a gladness that sorrow retrieves.

Responding Version.

179 CALL ALL TO SEE THE LIGHT. 11.

Ye children of light, now the morning proclaim;
Call all to the sight, till they joy in its name;
With opening eyes, as the mists from them roll.
The morn they will prize, and its glories extol.

Wide-spread o'er the sky, see its glories now wave!
The breaking mists fly, and in sunlight we lave;
Awaking "creation," beginning to sing,
Joys in the salvation the morning doth bring.

Man sees that his God ever honors each son;
That, kin to the clod, he is sharing the "throne;"
And, while well unfolding his angelhood germ,
Is proudly beholding, he links with the worm.

In our opening day we can worship aright
The wisdom-display of the infinite might;
Can see that its blessings all-conquering prove,
And know that unceasing is infinite love.

Old H. in Res. Ver.

180 THE GOD WE WORSHIP. 11.

Our God is no "king," but all-glorious Love;
We worship his life-work below and above;—
In labor-devotion we joyfully praise
The soul of all being, the light of our days.

Resistless the might of the indwelling grace
Supplied by that fount to the infinite space;—
A jet of that fountain is every form,
Where grace, well evolving, outrides every storm:

In law's perfect care, ever seeking the light,
Unfolding, each nature maintains its own right:
Our follies all teach, and our blunders make plain
Our pathway through hells, till our heaven we obtain.

Response.

---

181 BEGONE, UNBELIEF.

11. *Tune—Christ in the Vessel.*

Begone, unbelief! for the morning is here—
Great Nature's relief from the bondage of fear;—
Old dogmas may wrestle, but light will inform;
Our tempest-tost vessel will master the storm.

Tho' clouds vail the day, yet her wisdom shall guide;
Our natures obey all the laws that provide;—
Tho' hopes may seem broken and fancies all fail,
Great Nature hath spoken, her word will prevail.

The creed-power is past e'er forbidding to think;
Mists breaking at last, trouble never can sink;
The soul's "Ebenezer" will doctrines review,
Learn Nature's good pleasure and help us all through.

True faith, thus, will save, for its light on our path
Will free every slave to old fancies of "wrath;"—
At last 'twill have taught us; and faith in the name
Of Nature, who wrought us, will lift us from shame.

No more we complain of the childish distress—
"Temptations" and pain, from "the creeds" growing less;
The *real* salvation, through Nature's true word,
Sweeps off tribulation, revealing her Lord.

Now all that we meet we find works for our good,
The bitter makes sweet and well fitted for food;

Birth, painful at present, will triumph erelong;
And then, O how pleasant faith's conquering song.

Responding Version.

---

182 FAITH'S FOUNDATION. 11.

How firm a foundation doth Nature afford
For faith; in her laws, in her workings, her word;
What more could her love unto us have made known
Than that in each soul she hath centered her throne?

In every condition and stage of our life;
In infancy's heedless and impulsive strife;
In youth's blundering reasoning and passion's control,
Her power on toward ripeness still carries the soul.

Fear not when "temptations" shall o'er thee prevail!
For lessons of wisdom thy follies unvail;
And the seeming "demon" that "leads thee astray,"
Is heaven's kind angel revealing thy way.

When vainly resisting, compelled, thou shalt go
Into seeming gulfs of "sin," darkness, and "woe,"
The "waters so dreadful and deep," thou wilt prove
Mere fogs, which distorted perception and love.

E'en then, toward the light of thy nature's true day
Thy passion-vitality forces the way.
And life's cleansing stream every blight shall efface,
And nourish the soul with developing-grace.

And thy fiery trials shall only refine
The gold of thy nature—the virtue divine;
Tho' painful the while are the flames' wasting-power,
They only the drosses of manhood devour.

And when, in old age, nature's workings shall
prove
Its ripened maturity's fullness of love,
Then life's flowing stream will be checked never-
more
By pebble-obstructions that lie on the shore.

The soul that on Nature has learned to repose
Will not find her forces to him proving foes;
That soul ne'er for dogmas its faith can forsake;
Its perfect foundation they never can shake.

Responding Version.

---

183 TRUE FAITH SERENE AMID CONFUSIONS. 11.

Mid scenes of confusion and folly's complaints,
The soul knowing Nature ne'er trembles nor faints;
He finds at her banquet of love there is room;
He knows that with her he is ever at home.

When passion's wild billows around him doth rage,
And loves turned to hatreds, in warfare engage,
He knows these, exhausted by folly's wild roam,
Reacting, will seek for their nature's true home.

His soul, no more chilled with dark fancies, of
"sin"
Knows heaven through these blunders at length
he shall win;
And that to his aid all his fellows will come,
While here he is building a heavenly home.

His faith on her laws, now, well grounded and
sure,
He works, through her aid, every joy to secure;
And tho' sorrow-waves may dash o'er him their
foam,
He still gains a foretaste of heaven—his home.

Responding Version.

184 COMFORT DIVINE. 10, 11.

O comfort divine, to know I am thine,
Kind Nature, to see thine own life serving mine!
I joy in thy name, thy grace freely claim,
And find its abundance is ever the same.

True pleasures abound; in rapture profound
I see their profusion as light opens round.
In morning's full glow we fully shall know
That heaven is with us, unfolding below.

O joyous foretaste of the heavenly feast!
Faith yearns for its fullness, and toward it would
haste:
Its flavor I prove, and thus onward I move
To the soul-filling banquet of heavenly love.

Response.

---

185 "CREEDS" NO MORE NEEDED.

10, 11.

O preach me no more the dark "creeds" of yore;
The time for such fancies with me now is o'er;
The light flowing round illumines the ground,
And truth undistorted I freely have found.

The souls that receive find light will relieve
From fears in which all darkened natures must
live.
My soul, cast away whate'er would delay,
Rise! scale now the mountains and meet the glad
day!

No dark one can know what light can bestow—
What joy, strength, and comfort within it doth
flow;—
Here fully I prove the heaven above
United to earth in the fullness of love:

Love's labor doth win old "death," "hell," and
"sin;"
Transforming, they help build a heaven within:
With rapture I cry: I rise! never die!
I live in the infinite love, ever nigh!

In daybeams I find that ever are joined
Our God and his children, no soul left behind:
To all of our race flows freely his grace,
And all in great Nature may see our Lord's face.

His laws' perfect care all kindred do share;
Their blessings find those who to ask never dare.
See! each open eye, see clustering nigh
His graces divine in a fullness-supply.

Responding Version.

---

186 FAREWELL TO A FRIEND DEPARTED.

Tune—Scotland.

Thou art gone to the grave, but we do not deplore
thee;
No sorrows nor darkness encompass the tomb;
Kind Nature hath shed through its portals, before
thee,
The light of her truth, which dispels all the gloom.

Thou art gone to the grave, we no longer behold
thee,
Nor tread the rough paths of the world by thy
side,
But the bright fields of angel life, spreading, in-
fold thee,
And we shall soon pass through the door opening
wide.

Thou art not in the grave, and its mansion forsaking,

Perchance thy weak spirit in doubt lingered long,
But the sunshine of heaven beamed bright on thy
waking,
And the sound thou didst hear was a welcoming
song.

Thou art risen from the grave, and the light flowing o'er thee,
Earth's fogs all dispersing, will prove a sure
guide,
And from earthly blunders and sorrows restore
thee,—
Old "death" hath no sting! for nought living
e'er died!

Responding Version.

---

187 WELCOME TO A NEW-BORN CHILD.

Tune—Scotland.

Thou art born to our life, and, while fond ones
caress thee,
Earth's shadowing sorrows disturb thy repose;
Yet, in first endeavors 'gainst "ills" that distress
thee,
Young faith labors ably for room mid its woes.

Thou art born to our life, earnest strife is before
thee—
Great toil if thine efforts secure thee a field
Where, free from the blight superstition sheds o'er
thee,
A full human ripeness thy earth-life may yield.

Thou art born to our life; in the terrible raking
Of passion's wild conflicts, perchance thou may'st
long
Find faith's weakened eye its great pole-star mis-
taking,
Till life's truest conquests seem triumphs of
"wrong."

Yet this is no life of mere purposeless sorrow—
The tempests develop the powers they employ:
The storm-day will pass, and a glorious morrow
Shall ripen, and give perfect fullness of joy.
Counterpart of "Farewell to a Friend Departed"

---

188 AWAKE FROM ALL DREAMING AND FEAR. 8. *Tune—Contrast.*

Awake from all dreaming and fear,
The light of the morning has come,
And brightly around us appear
Truth's angels, encircling our home.
We see, now, the vapors remove,
And this our terrestrial abode,
Responding to light from above,
Revealing the life of its God.

Our stumblings will soon have an end,
For morning full light will afford—
The fogs, as they break and ascend,
Will glow with the light of our Lord.
From all deadening vapors then clean,
Disease will not lurk in the air;
And fancies of "evil" and "sin"
The power of the truth will repair.

Our eyes, as they open, behold
Already the morning is here;—
That decking in silver and gold
The rising cloud-vapors appear:
Mid old superstitions, the grace
Of social-life conqueror stands,
And forces their builders to praise
Its power, and obey its commands.

The early creed-fancies' display
No more give our senses a light;—

We need not the torches—'tis day!—
  They pale and soon fade from our sight.
The fogs all dispersing, the skies
  Will in the full sunlight appear;
Ye dreamers, of darkness, arise!
  Awake! for the morning is here!

Response.

---

189 THE JOYOUS HOURS IN OPEN LIGHT. 8. *Tune—Contrast.*

How joyous, enlivening, the hours
  When Morning's clear light I can see—
Adversity-gloom, which "devours,"
  Has ceased to be gloomy to me!—
The storms of mid-winter in vain
  Would hinder the brilliant display;
The tempests but add to the train
  Of beauties that beam on my way;

The pestilent stench yields perfume,
  And soul-music huskiest voice,
And all jarring discords attune
  To harmony while I rejoice;
All trouble inspires, and each sigh
  Is zephyr with health on its wings,
While, like summer clouds flitting by,
  All sorrow new brightness soon brings.

Content darkest "woes" to embrace,
  And see them to pleasures refined—
To know that what seems to efface
  But gives larger light to my mind,
I would in thy rays ever move,
  With trouble expanding to cheer;
And heed not the wealth-toys which prove
  To soul-darkened natures so dear.

Yes, Nature, indeed I am thine!
  Thy love is the theme of my song!

I never can languish nor pine;
  Thy tempests and storms are not long:
When clouds of dark creeds vail the sky,
  And whirlwinds of prejudice roar,
I know they pass rapidly by,
  And nature's true balance restore.
Response.

---

190 SALVATION, AND WORKING WITH JESUS. 8. 6 l.

What mean these strange, excited throngs,
And sudden fervor of their songs,
I asked, do they behold the day,
And for its labors thus array?
"We seek salvation," they reply,
"The love of Jesus ere we die."

Is this the Jesus, I inquired,
Of Nazareth, the soul-inspired,
Who for the weak in sadness wrought
Till tyrants on him vengance brought?
"The same," the surging crowds reply,
"We seek his favor ere we die."

Then ye are those I long have sought,
I said, for, lo! in pain I've wrought
Some aid to gain to rescue those
Whom greedy tyrants plunge in woes!
"We seek for *heaven*," the crowds reply,
"*His saving grace* before we die."

We'll join, I said, and crush the power
Of those who would "his lambs" devour—
We'll superstition's gloom displace,
And shed heaven's light upon our race.
With pious wrath they all reply,
"*Shall we forget our God and die!*"

I said we best shall God obey
As Jesus wrought and led the way—

In saving man from present woes;
That man's oppressors were *his foes.*
"*Ye Infidel!*" the crowds reply,
"*Put man before our God, and* DIE!"

Disheartened now, I turned away;
And then I saw a few array,
With Jesus, in the armor, bright,
Of love fraternal, for the right;
And faith and hope to doubts reply:
"We'll save our race! It shall not die!"
Response to a "Revival Hymn."

---

191 TYRANNY IS FALLING.

Tune—Old Hymn—"Babylon is Fallen."

Hail the day so long expected—
  Dawning day of full release—
When, from lawless "laws" protected,
  Human nature gains its peace!—
Sounding through all lands and nations,
  Freedom's judgment-trumpets roar:
Tyranny is falling! falling! falling!
  Tyanny is falling to rise no more!

Hail, ye long-desponding toilers,
  Now uprising, in your might,
To o'erthrow the world's despoilers
  And enthrone eternal right!—
Ye shall gain your own true stations,
  Conquering all that stands before:
Tyranny is falling! falling! falling!
  Tyranny is falling to rise no more!

Hail, ye dauntless champions, facing
  Scorn, and all reproach, to free
From a slavery "disgracing"
  For a true humanity!—
Persecution skulks behind you;
  Honors beckon just before:

Tyranny is falling! falling! falling!
  Tyranny is falling to rise no more!

Pharisaic "moral-magnates"
  Smite each other's cherished fame;
All their vaunted "virtue" stagnates,
  And their "honors" turn to shame:
Shrinking from the light increasing,
  "Saintly robes" protect no more:
Tyranny is falling! falling! falling!
  Tyranny is falling to rise no more!

Freedom's friends their feelings hiding,
  Seeking popular renown,
Find pretense, their champions chiding,
  But secures the public frown—
Zeal in slurring freedom's leaders
  Favor lost doth not restore:
Tyranny is falling! falling! falling!
  Tyranny is falling to rise no more!

Despots ask, in haughty madness,
  "What is this that comes to pass?"
Then, in deepening tones of sadnes,
  Murmer, "Oh! alas! alas!"
Hear them cry, in deep vexation,
  "All our days of power are o'er—
Tyranny is falling! falling! falling!
  Tyranny is falling to rise no more!"

See! the rays of truth are fiering
  Wrongs usurping virtue's name;
Let the people, never tiring,
  Clap their hands and blow the flame!—
Now begins a new creation—
  The old systems's day is o'er—
Tyranny is falling! falling! falling!
  Tyranny is falling to rise no more!

Responding Version.

192 THE GLORY OF NATURE AND OF MAN. 8. 7.

Now, through every land and nation,
Comes the glimmering dawning rays
Of the day of new "creation;"
Manhood's day of labor-praise.
While the dawning deepens, nature
Opens to the wondering thought,
As divine unfolding-power
Into forms of beauty wrought.

Thus the providence, that governs
Through the infinite domain,
Dwells in angels, in the sparrow,
In each living thing doth reign.
There from falls it works redemptions—
Bears unfolding life along
Till it, ripening, gives expression
To the grandest seraph-song.

Then it sees the Father's glory
In evolving earth and sky;
Sees that this and Mother's beauty
Are forever—never die.
Well may angels, all around us,
To the dawn devote their lays;
None beholding e'er, ungrateful,
Can withhold responding praise.

Once beheld, the opening glory
Sends its beams through every "woe,"
And reveals to every captive,
Soul-releasing power in flow:
For an all-sufficient saviour
Morning shows, whose highest throne
Is the human heart, forever
True to laws which are its own.

Response.

193 NATURE'S TRIUMPHANT LEAD. 8. 7.

Everywhere kind Nature leads us;
  What have we to ask beside?
All around, and here within us,
  Nature's laws our footsteps guide.
What tho', in our childish efforts,
  Pain from stumbles oft proceeds?
Thus her law-within is gaining
  Light for equilibrium-needs.

Everywhere kind Nature leads us—
  Well embodied here in man
Are her laws, in germ-unfolding;
  Here the God that shapes the plan:
'Sins"—our crude mistakes—are serving
  As the monitors, to teach,
Till, in manliness completed,
  Wisdom's balance we shall reach.

Everywhere kind Nature leads us
  On toward life of manly joy:
Tho' disturbing life-conditions
  Present pleasures may alloy,
Nature's vital force, within us,
  Struggles till the "woe" has passed,
And, triumphant, will secure us
  Harmony—a heaven—at last.

Response.

---

194 ONWARD, UPWARD, NATURE'S FREEMEN. 8. 7.

Onward! Upward! Nature's freemen;—
  Never more, in meekness, herd
Where old dogma-mists can blind you,
  Hiding Nature's written word!
In the deepening light of morning
  Nature's God and Law appear.

Clearly seen, their smiling features
  Banish superstition-fear.
Onward! scale life's mountain regions,
  Where the fogs all disappear.

Onward! Upward! still reflecting
  Light upon the vales below;
Aiding all advancing fellows
  To repulse the threatening foe;
In the opening light, surveying
  Error's forces 'neath your feet,
And their weakness well perceiving,
  Fearless ye their shafts can meet;
Ye will see their breaking forces,
  Panic-stricken, soon retreat.

Onward! till our race is rescued
  From old superstition's power;
Till its darkened, greedy minions
  Timid souls no more devour:
When ye boldly push the conflict
  And pursue them to the light,
Error's armies must surrender
  To your truth-supported might;
And, with you their forces joining,
  Serve the cause of truth and right.

Response.

---

195 CALL THEM IN, WHOE'ER IS NEEDY.

8. 7.

Call them in, whoe'er is needy,
  To the bounty freely spread
By our loving Mother Nature;
  Fully here may all be fed;
Call them in, the dogma-darkened,
  Tortured by the sense of "sin;"
Now the opening light of morning
  They are craving;—call them in.

Call them in, the Jew and Gentile,
  All, the greatest and the least,
Bid their hungry, famished spirits
  Come to Nature's gospel feast;
Superstition's victims, groping
  With their soul-supplies unseen,
To the all-suffient banquet
  Freely bid them;—call them in.

Call them in, the "saints," "professors,"
  Starving on their "pious" pride,
While our God and Nature's worship—
  Soul religion—they deride;
Call them with the poor and wretched,
  Plundered by their "pious" "sin;"
They will make full restitution
  When enlightened;—call them in.

Call them in, the drooping-hearted,
  Cowering 'neath the brand of "shame,"
Which, for love's divinest worship,
  Creedlings put on lovers' name;
Let all victims of oppression,
  In the opening light, begin
All their wants to fully honor;—
  All the needy, call them in.

Response.

---

196 LET US BASK WITHIN THE SUNBEAMS. 8. 7,

Let us bask within the sunbeams
  Of our nature's opening day,
Grasp the countless proffered blessings
  Which the morning gleams display:
With the light thus flowing o'er us,
  We may gather roses sweet
While the thorns may never wound us,
  Never pierce the wandering feet.

All our world abounds with treasures,
  Freely offered for our use;
All her many dreaded "evils"
  Come from blunders and abuse:
Through the darkness of the ages
  Of old superstition's night,
Her best joys were rarely gathered;
  Oft, abused, were made to blight.

Human energies thus working,
  Hindered, struggling, turned to greed;
Love fraternal, hurt by blunders,
  Soured, and caused the race to bleed;
Greed enslaved to gather treasures;
  Loves the passions fierce became
When the blinded morals, groping,
  Sought to curb by curse and blame.

But within the flowing sunbeams
  Of our science-lighted day
We may pluck the blooming roses
  While thorns we turn away.
Let us bask within the glories
  Of our nature's morning light;
Turn to blessings all the "evils"
  Of old superstition's night.

Counterparting Response.

---

197 OUR SECURITY. 8. 7.

Glorious things by thee are spoken,
  Nature, consort of our God!
And thy word can ne'er be broken;
  Here we have a safe abode:
On the rock eternal founded,
  We have found secure repose;
With thy law of life surrounded
  There can be no conquering foes.

Ever streams of living waters,
  Springing from eternal love,
Well supply thy sons and daughters;
  Full, abundant, ever prove.
Who can faint when such a river
  Freely all his thirsts assuage?
Grace from nature's God, the giver,
  Never fails from age to age.

Round each habitation hovering,
  God and Nature's laws appear,
Nerving human powers, and covering
  When a danger passes near.
Reason's light upon our banner
  Is defense by night and day;
Works for us in perfect manner;
  Teaches how to truly pray.

Responding Version.

---

198 LOVE DIVINE. 8. 7.

Love Divine, all love impelling,
  Joy of heaven, its life's renown,
Evermore, within us dwelling,
  All our lives with wisdom crown:
Father, Mother, Vital Spirit,
  Love's unbounded life thou art!
Let us more thy love inherit;
  Fill to fullness every heart.

Let thy light, so well beginning
  From the mists to set us free,
Fully save from fear of "sinning"
  In our strife for liberty:
Let it show that only blessings
  Thy severest judgments prove;
That but kindly love-caressings
  Are thy powers, below, above.

Let, oh, let life's richest treasure
  Overflow from every breast,

Filling earth with heavenly pleasure,
  Giving souls divinest rest:
Come, almighty to deliver!
  Strife and darkness then will flee,
And the earth, matured, shall ever
  Yield the fruits of harmony.

Then, in ever-new creation,
  Life shall flow in labor-prayer,
And our souls, complete salvation
  Find in thine abundant care:
Then in real, crowing glory
  Man shall stand; and earth shall blaze,
While it joins with heaven, before thee,
  In all nature's concert-praise.

Responding Version.

---

199 NATURE, FOUNT OF EVERY BLESSING. 8, 7.

Nature, fount of every blessing,
  Tune my heart to sing thy grace;
Streams of bounties, free, unceasing,
  Call for songs of earnest praise:
Teach me some melodious sonnet,
  That my soul may rise above
Every care that weighs upon it;
  Joyous in thy perfect love.

Then I'll raise my Ebenezer;
  Hither by thy help I'm come;
Knowing that each needed treasure
  Nature strews around my home.
Nature found me when a ranger,
  Plunged in superstition's flood;
Then she rescued me from danger;
  On her firm foundation stood.

To her Morning light a debtor
  Ever I'm constrained to be!

May it soon break every fetter,
  And from superstition free:
Prone to wander, oft, I feel it,
  Prone to leave the light I love;
Fully to my soul reveal it;
  Then triumphant it will prove.

Responding Version.

---

200 MORNING GOSPEL. 8, 7. 6 l.

Now the truth-exploring spirit
  Sees, responding to its need,
Grace divine, which all inherit;
  Fully able all to feed·
This is gospel, Morning gospel,
  Hungry souls supply your need!

O that all were now possessing
  All the fullness Nature gives!—
Knew that this, her perfect blessing,
  Every open hand receives!
Then would never life-endeavor
  Lack the fullness that she gives.

Response.

---

201 PARTING FROM A SOCIAL CIRCLE.

8, 7 6 l

As we part, let Nature's blessing
  Give us perfect joy and peace,
Knowing that we are posessing
  All her loving law of grace.
This refreshes, well refreshes,
  For our lives' unfinished race.

Grasp her work with adoration
  For her gospel truth profound,

That the laws of our salvation
In our nature's lives abound;
And be faithful, ever faithful
To the truth we here have found.

Thus our lives, to labor given,
In our mother Nature's way,
May create on earth a heaven,
Where no sorrow dims the day.
Let us ever well endeavor
Truth to give its perfect sway.

Responding Version.

---

202 NATURE'S WORD OF PROMISE.

8, 7.

All my darkening doubts have vanished!
Nature's voice mine ears have heard;
There I read life's loving promise—
There our Mother's sacred word.

CHORUS.—Thus I'm trusting, fully trusting
In the promise I have heard;
In the all-perfecting power
Which our Mother's laws afford.

All my dread of "sin" has vanished!
In the light mine eyes perceive
"Sin" is but the blundering vigor
Which, when wise, will all retrieve,

CHO.—Thus I'm trusting, etc.

All my chilling fears have vanished!
For I know that Nature's power—
All her laws—protecting forces,
Work within me every hour.

CHO.—Thus I'm trusting, etc.

Joy prevails, the sorrows vanish,
And their dwindling shadows fade;

For the God within is master,
Giving every needful aid.

CHO.—Thus I'm trusting, etc.

All I am, with darkness vanished,
Joins with the creative soul;
Nature's laws and forming spirit
Will eternally control.

CHO.—Thus I'm trusting, etc.

Response.

---

203 LOOK, O BROTHERS! 8, 7, 4.

Look, O brothers! Morning greets you!
Lovingly her daybeams fall!
Free, abounding, and unceasing,
"Open wide your eyes!" they call:
Look, O brothers!
Then will dwindling creeds grow small.

Haste, O brothers, toward the regions
Of the clearer opening day!
When its beaming grace flows o'er you
Morbid fears will pass away:
Haste, tho' stumbling,
You must stumble while you stay.

Response.

---

204 MORNING GOSPEL'S MESSAGE.

8, 7, 4. *Tune—Greenville, or Nettleton.*

Anxious souls, now hear the message
Morning brings of light and love;
Every sentence offers blessings;
E'en its threatenings teem with love:
Listen to it!
E'en its threatenings teem with love:

Long you've hungered for a gospel—
News of gladness to the soul;
Now it comes in Morning's teachings,
Scattering mists which round us roll.
O how cheering
To the long-desponding soul.

Hear it, "All your 'sins' are saviours;"
Fearful hearts now quell your fears:
"Tempted" souls, they bring you succor—
Pains are monitors, to cheer,
Kindly aiding
To instruct and give you cheer.

"The long-dreaded 'demon'—'evil,'
Is an angel, ever true,
Which our God makes sole conductor—
Blunders teach and help you through;—
Hells are transient;
Blunders teach and help you through.

"Not a 'miracle of mercy,'
Contravening Nature's laws,
But *your nature's life evolving*,
Wisdom cures your folly-flaws;"
Hear the gospel—
"*Wisdom* cures your folly-flaws."

Responding Version.

---

205 IT IS FINISHED.

8, 7, 4. *Tune—Greenville, or Nettleton.*

It is finished—night is closing—
Superstition-shades withdraw;
Frightful dreams of "God avenging,"—
"Death" and "hell," no more shall awe:
It is finished!
All from this may comfort draw.

Tune your harps ye sons of Morning!
  Tune them for the joyous theme
Of a God through nature ruling,
  Now beheld, in Morning's gleam,
    Shedding blessings
  In an all-suppylying stream.

Response.

---

206 MORNING GOSPEL'S CALL.

8, 7, 4. *Tune—Greenville, or Nettleton.*

Come ye superstition-victims,
  With desponding struggles sore,
Morning light is flowing round you,
  Full of soul-illuming power:
    Fully able,
  Fully willing; doubt no more.

Every needy soul is welcome
  To the flowing light-supplies;
See! how easy the condition—
  Only open wide your eyes:
    Then enlightened,
  Free, "redeemed," your souls shall rise.

Let not conscience make you linger
  With its morbid fitness-dream,
Morning gospel but requireth
  Want receptive to its beam:
    This, within you,
  Works as aspiration's gleam.

Come ye weary dogma-laden,
  Dreaming of a hopeless fall,
Nature's Morning Gospel, better,
  Offers freely joy to all,
    Through its righteous
  Law of light's resistless call

Agonizing for a "pardon"
  While your darkened spirits lie,
Nature's God his light is sending
  In unfailing joy-supply.
    This will finish
  Fear, and show you heaven is nigh.

God within you is ascending—
  Aspiration moves your blood;
Venture on him! venture wholly!
  Let no groundless fear intrude:
    This, your Saviour,
  Will secure all needed good.

Men and angels, now in concert,
  Join to praise the loving name
Of our nature's God, whose justice
  To his child imputes no blame:
    Look! ye fearful;
  Look! and ye may join the same.

Responding Version.

Note—Omitting the last two lines of each stanza, we may sing with the above this CHORUS: *Tune—"Turn to the Lord."*

Turn to the light and find salvation
  From the fears that rack and pain!
Here is full, complete salvation:
  Peace and joy within it reign.

Response.

---

207 WORSHIP IN THE MORNING LIGHT.

7.

Nature's God, we see thee now!—
We no more with trembling bow,
For we know our fears were vain;
That no suit thou wilt disdain.

Nature's God, we know thee friend;
Know thy blessings never end;
And thy ever-flowing grace
Tunes our lips to sing thy praise.

In thine own true, working way
We would ever truly pray;
Thus we see, where'er we go,
Thou thy blessings wilt bestow.

Every view thy works afford
Gives some message of thy word;
Aids thy lessons to impart,
And with love to warm the heart.

When in superstition-mist,
Still thy life did us assist—
Every impulse did impel
'Gainst life-hamperings to rebel.

Freed at last, we know thee now,
And no more with trembling bow,
For we know our fears were vain;
That no suit thou wilt disdain.

Responding Version.

---

208 GROUNDS FOR PERSEVERANCE

7.

Now, in Morning light, we sing
Liberty that knows no king;
Nature's children, we can praise
All her glorious works and ways.

We have found our nature's God
Where our fathers stumbling trod;
They in mists were struggling, we
Through the thinning vapors see.

Thus our souls, no more afraid,
Find no foes our path invade—

"Demons" of the mists become
Brothers of our nature's home.

Fearless then we forward go,
For we find, above, below,
Nature's laws will leader be,
And we follow joyfully.

Response.

---

209 NATURE OUTWORKS RIGHTEOUSNESS. 7.

Morning comes! the waking soul
Finds the mists before him roll;
Sees that God and Nature's grace
Works in all for righteousness:

Learns there is no "inbred sin;"
Hears their laws command, "Be clean;"
Sees befoulments all remove,
Cleansed by the unfolding love;

Sees her laws, as God desires,
Yield whatever man requires;
That to his own hands they've given
Power to build himself a heaven.

Response

---

210 COME, MY SOUL, TO PRAYER. 7.

Come, my soul, thy suit prepare,
Nature always answers prayer,
Real prayer—the earnest play
Of our powers in nature's way.

Nature, more than priest or king,
Full supplies to all can bring;
And, her flowing grace is such,
None can ask, aright, too much.

Then, O Nature, I begin:
Freedom ask from sense of "sin;"
Power to see our nature's right
Thus to blunder on to light.

On thy loving laws I call,
Knowing they suffice for all,
And, within their free control,
Serve the body and the soul.

Oh, within the dawning day,
Teach me how to truly pray
Labor-prayer, which well supplies
Blessings free from earth and skies!

Then each spring of life shall send
Prayer and praise, whose streams shall blend;
Wisdom's labor all shall be,
Which co-operates with thee.

Responding Version.

---

211 ROCK OF AGES. 7. 6 l.

Rock of ages—Law Divine—
Nature's Law, thy strength is mine!
Firmly now I stand on thee;
From the dogma-quicksands free,
While old superstition raves,
Dashing round her fiercest waves.

Here, within the dawning day,
Blinding mists all melt away;
Superstition-fears give place
To the faith in Nature's grace;
"Sins" I see mistakes alone,
For which Nature's laws atone.

Nothing more of strength I need,
E'en tho' envy, mammon, greed,

Despot forces all combine,
Thinking thee to undermine;
Firm, undaunted, I remain,
Knowing all their strength is vain.

On, at duty's every call,
I will move, and fear no fall,
And, tho' yielding up my breath,
Triumph o'er illusive "death;"
Rock of ages—Law Divine—
Nature's Law, thy strength is mine!

Responding Version.

---

212 MORNING WARMS OLD DOGMA'S CHAMPIONS. 7. 6 l.

Dogma's champions, you relent!—
  Mists dissolve in daybeams' flood,
And the "holy zeal" is rent
  Which would shed the "doubters" blood:
What has love fraternal done?
  O'er your creeds a victory won!

Now your brother-hand would feed
  Those who slight your God and "prayer;"
Persecution, to succeed,
  Plays deception everywhere;
And the despot-skill supplies
  Victims few for sacrifice.

Your old "morals" die! in vain
  Would your souls revere their word;
The old "duties" give you pain;
  Human love has these ignored;
Thought, befogged, scarce plays its part,
  But a daybeam finds your heart.

Give it room! oh, give it play!
  It will warm your present hours,

And, for fuller opening day,
  Strengthen all your manhood powers!
Then, from false ideals free,
  God in darkest souls you'll see.

Response.

---

213 BROTHERS, TURN! 7.

Brothers, turn; why will ye try
From the light to hide the eye?
Brother, light is seeking thee—
Seeking all from fogs to free—
To release from morbid fears,
Superstition's woes and tears;
Why, ye blinded brothers, why
Will ye to avoid it try?

Brothers, turn; why will ye try?
Nature's God is asking why;
He within your souls desires
New supplies to vital fires;—
All the manhood-nature craves
Light, which from soul-dwarfing saves;
Why, ye needy brothers, why
Will ye to avoid it try?

Turn! oh, turn! why will ye try?
All your wants are asking why;
All your sorrows, all your fears,
All your hopes of manly years;—
Reason's morning light, in flow,
Nature's God would make you know;
Why, ye darkened brothers, why
Will ye to avoid it try?

Response.

---

214 NATURE, MOTHER OF MY SOUL. 7.

Nature, Mother of my soul,
  Let me on thy bosom lie

When the surging waters roll,
  While life's tempest rages high:
Guide me, glorious Mother, guide
  When the storms are sweeping past;
Then from duty ne'er I'll hide,
  But the helm control at last.

Other reffuge have I none;
  I no other need but thee;
Let, oh let thy life enthrone
  Manly energy in me!
All the help my nature needs
  To my aid thy working brings,
Till my growing soul succeeds
  In developing its wings.

Plenteous help in thee is found
  To illumine all within,
Showing truth and love abound,
  Freeing from the dream of "sin."
Shed, oh shed it over all,
  Till they know their natures pure,
And old superstition's thrall
  Shall no more on earth endure!

Responding Version.

---

215 LITANY CHANGED TO LIGHT. 7.

Nature, when on bended knee
We were bowing, scorning thee,
When, "repentant," to the skies
Manhood lifted streaming eyes;
For his life's divinest flow
Fearing an "avenging foe,"
Nature's life thy soul-supply
Changed to light our litany.

By thy law, which, through all years,
Joy evolves from griefs and fears,

Making every brief distress
Help from folly's wilderness;
Making dreaded "tempter's" power
Give us victory every hour,
Till our souls are lifted high
From old dogmas' litany:

By the conflicts with despair
Of our souls' unconscious prayer
While our blindness held, in scorn,
Manhood's life "depraved," "forlorn,"
By the crosses, thorns, and cries
Of the manhood-sacrifice,
Mists are driven from the eye—
Superstition's litany.

Every suffering creature's groan
Human nature makes its own;
Love fraternal strikes to save;
It will free each struggling slave;
Thus our nature's loving Lord
Ever will his aid afford—
Give our need's unconscious cry
Light instead of litany.

Response.

---

216 LOVE'S DIVINE LIFE PREVAILS. 7.

In our Morning's dawning light
  Prison walls we mount above,
For the senses opening sight
  Sees divine the life of love:
Powers of darkness, crying "stay,"
  Hydra-persecutions rear;
Dogma-cant and despot-sway
  Wake no overpowering fear:

Outworn, dying moralisms
  Strike no "reverential dread;"

Churchly power desolves in "schisms,"
  Manhood rises; lifts its head:
See! where outer thought assents
  To the code of monkery,
Intuition this resents,
  Strikes to make their natures free.

We would aid the opening powers;
  Helping them to act aright—·
Taming wildness which devours,
  By reflecting morning light;
We can join no darkening bands,
  Who would hide life's forming-cause;
We with reverential hands
  Touch the theme and teach the laws.

Vain we know the childish thought
  To promote morality,
Any real virtue sought,
  By withholding light to see:
Aspiration bravely strives
  While her efforts bruises yield;
Even then her virtue thrives;
  And at last it wins the field:

Nature's central love repressed,
  Finds, as vital powers increase,
That, as passion wild expressed,
  Bursting forth, it gives release:
Nature struggles till she gains
  Freedom's equlibrium flow;
Thus she harmony obtains—
  Thus creates a heaven below.

Response to "Moralistic" Persecutors.

---

217 MORNING MISSIONARY-HYMN. 7, 6.

Through all our highland regions
  Where daybeams light the skies,

Earth's weary, toiling legions
  Against their tyrants rise,
And, struggling to resist them,
  As light flows o'er the plains,
Call on us to assist them
  In striking off their chains.

What tho' with plenty, teeming,
  Our beauteous world o'erflows,
Greed, with its legal scheming,
  Spreads o'er it want and woes;
In vain with lavish kindness
  Fond Nature's wealth is strown
While, robbed and kept in blindness,
  The workman has no home.

Shall we, who know how blighting
  Is foul monopoly,
E'er cease to aid in fighting
  To set the people free?
Or heed the cynics ever
  Who, as "reformers," seek
To slur each true endeavor
  For freedom's cause to speak?

No! full emancipation
  To all the world declare,
Till through each land and nation
  Its echoes fill the air;
Till every honest toiler
  His rights shall fully gain,
And the would-be despoiler
  Shall ply his arts in vain.

Response.

---

218 ONE TRUE WORD FOR JESUS. 7, 6.

Now, one true word for Jesus,
  No cant of darkening creeds,

A word of recognition
  Of his true life and deeds

CHORUS.—A *truthful* word for Jesus;
    Proclaim it day by day
  To all the souls benighted,
    Who now his cause betray.

His doctrine—loving justice
  To all our human kind—
Preach loudly till it reaches
  The pharisaic mind.

CHO.—A *truthful* word, etc.

With manly zeal and courage,
  His gospel well proclaim,
Till despots cease oppressing
  Their fellows in his name.

CHO.—A *truthful* word, etc.

Declare it our first duty
  To break the cruel bands
Imposed by greed and priestlings
  On human hearts and hands.

CHO.—A *truthful* word, etc.

Indorse the words of Jesus,
  Which fully give to all
Respect, fraternal honor,
  However low they fall.

CHO.—A *truthful* word, etc.

Take up the cross of Jesus;
  Despise reproach and "shame,"
Which "pious" error's magnates
  Cast on you in his name.

CHO.—The *truthful* word for Jesus
    Speak boldly *every day*,
  Till error's victims, lighted,
    His law of love obey.

Response.

219 FEAR AT NATURE'S GOSPEL GATE.

6.

Before the open gate
  Of Nature's gospel, mild,
With trembling I did wait,
  Kind Nature's fearful child—
Oppressed with creed-taught fear
  Of "penalties" and "sin,"
Her voice I could not hear,
  Which bade me enter in.

Within the misty view,
  Our nature's God appeared
Distorted, dark, untrue,
  And greatly to be feared;
The smiling angels seemed
  "Malignant 'demon' foes,"
And morbid fancy dreamed
  Of "wrath" and "vengeful woes."

Awhile my spirit stood
  In superstition-plight,
Then came the dawning flood
  Of nature's Morning light;
I saw the "demon wiles,"
  Which seemed the "lures to 'sin,'"
Were beckoning angels' smiles,
  And, fearless, entered in.

I found our nature's God,
  And all his angel bands,
Instead of "vengeful rods,"
  Extended loving hands.
Thus, joying in their love,
  My soul in triumph sings,
And to the world would prove
  The truth the morning brings.

Response.

220 JOYING IN NATURE.

6, 9. *Tune—Rapture.*

O how happy are they
Who kind Nature obey,
And have learned to confide in her love!
O what tongue can express
The sweet comfort and peace
Which her laws in their harmony prove!

That sweet comfort is mine,
For the favor divine
I have found working there for my good;
And, content, I believe
Every "woe" 'twill retrieve,
And I bathe in the life-giving flood!

'Tis a heaven below
Nature's grace thus to know,
And the angels can do nothing more
Than its fullness to meet,
And in harmony sweet
The great Mother of All to adore.

O the glorious hight
Of the perfect delight
Which great Nature's clear light can afford!
Of its fullness possessed,
We can labor with zest,
And rejoice in the aid of her Lord.

Nature all the day long
Is the theme of my song;
O that all her clear light could but see!
Then, old creeds cast aside,
Perfect faith would abide,
And the natures of all would be free.

Responding Version.

221 THE FREE SOUL'S ASPIRATIONS.

6, 5.

More manliness give me—
  More vigor within—
To rise above suffering
  And fancies of "sin;"—
Let Reason—my Saviour—
  His light, love, and care,
Show Nature unfolding
  Full answers to prayer.

A larger faith give me
  To trust in our Lord—
His life, law, and glory,
  In Nature, his word;
That tears and vain sorrows,
  And all morbid grief,
In Nature's revealings
  May find their relief.

Full consciousness give me
  That all life is pure;
That ne'er on the spirit
  A stain can endure;
Then for thy great "kingdom"
  More fitted I'll be,
And find, loving Nature,
  A heaven with thee.

Response.

---

222 THIS WORLD IS NOT ALL FLEETING SHOW.

This world is not all fleeting show,
  For man's illusion given:
Who feels his heart with love aglow,
Dispelling fear, begins to know
  The true delights of heaven.

Who wakes to see our opening day,
With feelings calm and even
Beholding its sublime display
Of truth and beauty, well can say,
Earth hath the light of heaven.

Who looks with open eyes and mind,
Whence blinding mists are driven
And goblin fancies cast behind,
With joy unspeakable doth find
That this, our earth, is heaven.

Response.

---

223 THE VICTIM OF PLUNDER.

Tune—Exile of Erin.

There woke to the light the poor victim of plunder,
And lo! from his features soon vanished the chill
With which, long despairing, he had struggled under
The "laws" of old despots, who robbed him at will:
As the Day-Star in glory now rose o'er the ocean,
Its rays soon attracted his eyes' glad devotion;
And then, in the flow of new-kindled emotion,
He sang the bold anthem of justice for all.

"Tho' hard is my lot," said the poor wandering stranger,
"Despoiled and enslaved from the day of my birth,
I shall have a refuge from famine and danger—
The workman shall yet have a home on the earth!
Then never again shall his soul cringe and cower,
And bow to the despot, or yield to his power,
But in peace and plenty shall spend each sweet hour,
And sing in full freedom of justice for all.

"Ah! long have I dreamed of the day which is
nearing;
And long have I wondered if e'er it should be;
But, lo and behold! now its dawn is appearing!—
The workmen are rising in true majesty:
Hurrah! see their banners now proudly float o'er
us!
See! in wild dismay tyrants shrink from before
us,
While truth in her might now aids to restore us
The rights of the people—true justice for all."

Response

---

224 WORKMEN, ROUSE.

Tune—Bruce's Address.

Workmen, rouse! in every land,
Ye who toil with head or hand,
Sons and daughters, take your stand
If you would be free!

"Legal" robbers—men of prey—
Steal your heritage away
To support their pomp and sway:
This is slavery!

Who at their behest would toil—
Never once attempt to foil
Despots who their homes despoil,—
Let them bow the knee!

Who would battle for the right,
Who for equity would fight,
Let him rise! and, with his might,
Strike Monopoly!

Tho' in rage the tyrant raves,
Swear by all your martyred braves
You his meek, submissive slaves
Never more will be!

Banish plundering "laws" from earth,
And enthrone its real worth;
Give to every child, from birth,
  Perfect liberty!

Response.

---

225 RESCUE THE SUFFERING.

Rescue the suffering,
Seemingly "perishing,"
Ever assist the desponding to save;
Light give the erring one,
Lift up the fallen,
Teach them respect for the natures they have,

CHORUS.—Rescue the suffering,
  Seemingly "perishing,"
  Tho' you from Pharisees
  Censure receive.

Tho' in the deepest sloughs
Hopelessly sinking,
Loaded with scorn, disrespected by men,
Give them a brother's hand,
Lovingly aid them,
Then they will rise into manhood again.

CHO.—Rescue, etc.

Down in the darkest heart,
'Neath the stained surface,
Treasures lie burried that love can restore;
Touched by a loving hand,
Wakened by kindness,
Cords nearly broken will vibrate once more.

CHO.—Rescue, etc,

Rescue the suffering;
Duty demands it—

Duty to self—to the life of the soul;
Love, true fraternal love
Linked with our fellows,
Ever conducts to a heavenly goal.

CHO.—Rescue, etc.

Response.

---

226 THE JOYOUS TO-DAY.

Tune—The Sweet By-And-By.

Our old earth is as fair as the day,
Could we see, in the clear open light,
The divine love and wisdom display
Of our God in his up-building might.

CHORUS.—In the joyous to-day
We shall see when the fogs are no more;
In the joyous to-day
We shall see when the fogs are no more.

We shall sing when the fogs are no more;
When the dark lingering mists disappear;
We shall find that our sorrows are o'er;
We shall know that a heaven is here.

CHO.—In the joyous, etc.

Then, our earth fully ripened, the race
Shall no more go to war and destroy,
But, in Nature's developing-grace,
Love and wisdom their powers will employ.

CHO.—In the joyous, etc.

Then old "death" shall no more be a "foe,"
Who shall "rack us with harrowing pain,"
But shall kindly assistance bestow
Till the angelhood crown we obtain.

CHO.—In the joyous, etc.

Counterparting Response.

227 TAKE THE FORT.

Tune—Hold the Fort.

Comrades, see! the gray is spreading
O'er the Eastern sky!
Morning dawns, the fogs are breaking,
Light falls on the eye!

CHORUS.—Take the fort from error's forces;
Error's armor fails;
Superstition shrinks, retiring,
Morning light prevails!

Waking from their morbid dreaming,
Reason leading on,
Human souls are now perceiving
Error's power is gone.

CHO.—Take the fort, etc.

Nature's banner, see! 'tis streaming,
And her bugle-call
Soon shall waft triumphant music
To the ears of all.

CHO.—Take the fort, etc

Tho' it fiercely ruled for ages,
Superstition dies:
More and more the light is falling
On the open eyes.

CHO.—Take the fort, etc.

Response.

---

228 LIGHT COMES FLOWING ON.

Tune—John Brown.

Awaking manhood rises free from all its dreamy fear,
With senses opened freely Nature's truths to see and hear,

Withdrawing all its reverence from the creeds
that interfere
. As light comes flowing on.

CHORUS.—Glory, glory, hallelujah!
Glory, glory, hallelujah!
Glory, glory, hallelujah!
The light comes flowing on.

And tho' the priestly forces seek to bar the coming
day,
And on our morning prophets all their bigot-wrath
display,
Their prison walls no more suffice to hide the
deepening gray
As light comes flowing on.

CHO.—Glory, glory, etc.

In half-despairing efforts, persecution now must vail
Itself in false pretenses when the truth it would
assail;
Its weakening joints are showing through its borrowed coat of mail
As light comes flowing on.

CHO.—Glory, glory, etc.

We spurn its coward vengeance—we will boldly
take our stand
Against all lawless "legal" acts profaning freedom's land—
To manly courage branded "crime" we'll give the
cheering hand
As light comes flowing on.

CHO.—Glory, glory, etc.

We welcome home our martyr friends—the heroes
of to-day—
The conquerors that tho' in chains keep bigot-foes at bay,
And help us raise our eyes in joy to meet the
grand display
Of light now flowing on.

CHO.—Glory, etc. *Response.*

DOXOLOGIES.

---

1 L. M.

To nature's God let praises flow;
He dwells with man on earth below;
His reign is love—no monarch's throne;
His life in earth and heaven is one.

Response.

---

2 C. M.

Let God, the Father, Mother, Son,
  Be everywhere adored:
Their life in earth and heaven is one—
  The Human and its Lord.

Response.

---

3 C. M.

To Parent Soul and Human Child—
  The God whom we adore—
We give the homage of our souls,
  And shall for evermore.

Response.

---

4 C. M.

The God of nature be adored,
  Whose ever-forming breath
Speaks in her Law-Eternal word,
  Evolving life from "death:"
We praise the power which in the sun
  And earth is all divine—
All life, the high and low, is one,
  And men's with angels' join.

Response.

5 S. M.

Ye angels, long unknown,
  Now with us here below,
Your loving worship is our own ;
  Your converse now we know.

---

6 H. M.

To God our Father's throne—
  The human heart—we raise
The homage of each son,
  In lives of labor-praise :
Our every power to this we bring,
And heaven responds while thus we sing.
Response.

---

7 8. 7.

Praise the God who gives salvation,
  Through his law of boundless love
Working in us new creation—
  Making follies teachers prove—
Teachers giving explanation
  When our impulse-life would rove ;
Law Divine! our adoration
  All thy workings ever move.
Response.

END OF VOL. I.

www.ingramcontent.com/pod-product-compliance
Lightning Source LLC
Chambersburg PA
CBHW030823270326
41928CB00007B/875

* 9 7 8 3 3 3 7 2 6 5 7 6 2 *